THE COMPLETE GUIDE TO

Property Investment
IN FRANCE

Solely for convenience the terms 'he', 'him' and 'his'
have been used throughout this work. They should be
understood to include 'she' and 'her'.

THE COMPLETE GUIDE TO
Property Investment
IN FRANCE
A buy-to-let manual

GERRY FITZGERALD

howtobooks

Constable & Robinson Ltd
55–56 Russell Square
London WC1B 4 HP
www.constablerobinson.com

First published in the UK by How To Books
an imprint of Constable & Robinson Ltd, 2013

© 2013 Gerry FitzGerald

A copy of the British Library Cataloguing in
Publication Data is available from the British Library

ISBN 978-1-84528-448-0

Printed and bound by CPI Group (UK) Ltd, Croydon, CR0 4YY

1 3 5 7 9 10 8 6 4 2

Contents

Part Three: A Holiday Letting Business

Part Four: Long-term Letting

Part Five: Tax

Maps and Tables

Preface

For many in the UK the idea of buying a property in France summons up the image of a rustic cottage in Normandy or a farmhouse in the Dordogne – a bolt-hole, a retreat, cheap to buy, empty for most of the year and available for family and friends in the holiday season. There is little expectation of capital growth and no likelihood of a regular and growing income. This image, however, does not do justice to the reality of the French property market and the huge attractions it has for the serious investor.

There are two remarkable features of the property scene in France: its uniquely stable housing market and the sheer scale of its rental sector.

France, like other countries, was hit hard by the recession but its property market has emerged more bruised than battered from the crisis. While prices fell they didn't collapse and there was nothing like the scale of devastation – foreclosures, abandoned building sites, legions of empty new-builds – suffered by other countries (most notably Spain, Ireland and the UK).

The reason is simply that France declined to join the property boom and consequently avoided the property bust. Planning rules were not relaxed to accommodate developers. Mortgage lenders did not change their lending criteria to facilitate speculative purchases. Strict rules on affordability were maintained. They still exist. As a result, far fewer homeowners were forced to hand in their keys and widespread turmoil was avoided.

And what about buyer demand? The key factor here is affordability and, once again, the signs are positive. According to the National Association of French Estate Agents (FNAIM), property prices were as affordable for the average buyer in 2010 (taking income levels and interest rates into account) as they were in 2000. No change there.

When it comes to the rental sector France is uniquely placed in having both a thriving tourist industry and a vast long-term rental market.

France is the number one tourist destination in the world, with over 70 million visitors a year. Not surprisingly, there is always demand for affordable accommodation. In recent years cheap flights have fuelled this demand like never before. As a consequence, holiday letting has taken off, hugely facilitated by internet sites devoted exclusively to property owners in search of tenants.

An added bonus for the owner of a holiday let in France is that the property may qualify as a furnished holiday let for the purpose of UK tax. Qualifying properties have a variety of special tax benefits, including a capital gains tax rate as low as 10%!

With careful planning it is possible to own and enjoy that second home in France and, at the same time, make it pay.

As for the long-term rental market, the contrast with the UK is stark. For the French, renting is a way of life, with over 20% of the housing stock privately rented. The government, for its part (unlike its UK counterpart) regards the private rental sector as an asset, to be actively encouraged and supported. Tax concessions and incentive schemes of all sorts play a part. The long-term rental market is buoyant, with demand outstripping supply in most parts of the country.

As if all this weren't enough, property prices and mortgage interest rates are considerably lower than in the UK.

This book is the product of 12 years' experience in buying, managing and letting properties in France. The underlying principle is that the investment must pay for itself and meet the essential requirements of any buy-to-let purchase – a regular, reliable and growing income with a high expectation of long-term capital gain.

Welcome to Buy-to-Let France!

Gerry FitzGerald

Part One

WHERE TO BUY

For Holiday Letting

Holidaymakers in France are spoilt for choice. There is something unique in all the regions to make their stay the perfect holiday experience – from Nice, Cannes, Antibes and St Tropez in the Côte d'Azur to the ski slopes of Rhône-Alpes and the sandy beaches of Deauville in Normandy. So where to make a holiday let investment?

For a successful holiday letting business there is one essential requirement – a regular, reliable supply of holidaymakers eager and willing to rent. While all the regions of France attract tourists, some specific locations attract many more than others. This is due entirely to the phenomenal development of the low-cost airline industry.

HOLIDAY LET HOTSPOTS

The budget airlines have radically transformed the travel scene in Europe and the great majority of holiday let clients will reach their destination by using them. Indeed, the fierce competition from the no-frills sector has had the additional benefit of forcing national airlines to trim their fares and join in the fray. However wonderful a location might be in other respects, it will be at a great disadvantage if it is not close to an airport served by the low-cost airlines.

The following carriers currently operate from UK and Irish airports to destinations in France.

Table 1.1 Carriers serving holiday destinations in France

easyJet	Bmibaby	Sky South
Ryanair	Aer Arann	Aurigny
Flybe	German Wings	British Airways
Jet2	Air France	Aer Lingus

Airlines, however, can and do go out of business. Airlines can and do pull out of routes. What effect would either eventuality have on a holiday letting business? Given this inherent danger it is clearly important to know *how many* carriers fly to any particular French airport and from *how many* UK airports. Safety in numbers. There are wide discrepancies in the figures.

In the 'safest' category are those destinations which are served by five to eight carriers each from up to 20 UK and Irish airports (see Table 1.2). Next come those in the two to four carrier category (Table 1.3) and finally, those destinations served by only one airline (Table 1.4). These tables are, of course, a snapshot of the current position. Nothing stands still. Up-to-date research will be needed at the time of purchase.

BROADENING THE SEARCH

It is important to note that it is not only the immediate destination that benefits from the attention of the airlines. Nearby holiday locations are also served by the airport and properties in these areas can make excellent investments. Nice airport, for example, delivers holidaymakers to Cannes, Grasse, St Paul de Vence, Monaco, Monte Carlo, Villefranche, Cagnes-sur-mer and Antibes – all much sought after holiday destinations within easy reach of the airport.

For this reason Tables 1.2 and 1.3 below are accompanied not only by notes on the immediate destination but also by details of 'other destinations served by the airport'. These lists are based on properties currently available to rent on the main holiday letting websites (see Chapter 13), specifying the airport in question as the nearest to the property.

Table 1.2 First category holiday destinations

Destinations	Carriers	UK/Irish airports
Paris	8 + Eurostar	20
Nice	8	20
Marseille	7	12
Bordeaux	6	13
Toulouse	6	12
La Rochelle	5	11
Lyon	5	11

Paris

The most popular areas for holidaymakers are the Marais (4th *arrondissement*), the Latin Quarter around St Germain des Prés (6th), Montmartre (18th) and anywhere within striking distance of the Louvre and Nôtre Dame Cathedral. 'Striking distance', however, can also mean a short trip on the metro. It is a great deal cheaper to rent (and buy) in the Gare du Nord area (Eurostar

Map 1.1   First category holiday destinations

direct from London) and take the metro to the major attractions in just 15 minutes.

Nice (Alpes-Maritimes)

It is not difficult to see the tourist attraction of Nice – sun, sea and alfresco dining in the Cours Saleya as the stars twinkle over the Baie des Anges. It is host to festivals of all kinds throughout the year. While the Côte d'Azur as a whole is known to be expensive, Nice can cater for all budgets. Holidaymakers can choose a low cost studio in the Old Town or a luxury villa in Cimiez.

Other holiday destinations served by the airport
Cannes, Grasse, St Paul de Vence, Monaco, Monte Carlo, Ville-franche, Cagnes-sur-mer, Beaulieu-sur-mer, Antibes, Fayence, St Tropez.

Marseille (Bouches-du-Rhône)

The country's second largest city, linked to the capital by the high speed TGV train service, Marseille attracts weary Parisians and foreign tourists alike. Apart from various museums, attractions include glorious beaches, picturesque bays, scuba diving, wind surfing, boat trips to the Calanques and tours of the infamous prison fortress of Château d'If.

Other holiday destinations served by the airport
Cassis, Roquevaire, Carnoux-en-Provence, La Ciotat, Aubagne.

Bordeaux (Gironde)

Apart from its famous wine, tourist attractions include the Palais de la Bourse on the river Garonne, the Zoo de Bordeaux Pessac, the Musée d'Art Contemporain, the 11th century Cathédrale St André and paragliding on the nearby Dune de Pyla, the highest dune in Europe.

Other holiday destinations served by the airport
St Emilion, Libourne, Latresne, Merignac, Le Bouscat, Eysines and the Saintes, Royan and Jonzac areas of Charente Maritime.

Toulouse (Haute-Garonne)

Known as the *Ville Rose* because of the effect of the sunlight on the city's brick architecture, Toulouse is the country's fourth largest city. It is famous for its wine, cheeses, foie gras and unique Toulouse cassoulet. Tourist attractions include the Théatre Garonne, the Cathédrale St Étienne, the planetarium, the Paul Depuy Museum and the St Sernin basilica.

Other holiday destinations served by the airport
The *departments* of Tarn, Tarn-et-Garonne, Lot, Gers and the ski slopes of Ax les Thermes, Ascou Pailhères, Peyragudes and Saint-Lary Soulan.

La Rochelle (Charente-maritime)

La Rochelle is a delightful seaside resort, best know for its picturesque harbour and Old Town. Attractions include the Musée des Modèles Reduits (miniature models), Parc Ornithologique (nature reserve for wild birds), Musée Maritime Neptunea (see Jacques Cousteau's ship, Calypso) and Le Jam Pub (for jazz and blues fans).

Other holiday destinations served by the airport
Ile-de-Ré, La Rochelle-Surgères, Saint-Jean-d'Angely, Rochfort-Marennes, St Just, St Just Luzac, Deux-Sèvres, Montpellier De Medillan.

Lyon (Rhône)

France's third largest city, Lyon is considered the home of haute cuisine. Apart from the food, visitors are attracted by the Roman amphitheatres built by the Emperor Augustus, the Fourvière Basilica, the Parc des Hauteurs on the Fourvière Hill and the National Opera House. River cruises are available on the Rhône and Saône.

Other holiday destinations served by the airport
Pérouges, Monts du Lyonnais, St Romain-en-Gal, Crémieu and
the ski resorts of Alpe du Grand Serre, Autrans, Gresse en Vercors,
Lans en Vercors, Le Collet d'Allevard, Lelex, Mijoux-Lélax-la
Faucil, Prapoutel and Villard de Lans.

Table 1.3   Second category holiday destinations

Destinations	Carriers	UK/Irish airports
Nantes	4	10
Perpignan	3	10
Grenoble	3	8
Brest	3	6
Bergerac	2	13
Limoges	2	12
Rennes	2	11
Chambery	2	9
Dinard	2	6
Biarritz	2	5
Avignon	2	4
Montpellier	2	3

Nantes (Loire-Atlantique)

Sixth largest city in France and capital of the Pays de la Loire
region, Nantes has plenty to offer the visitor. It is host to jazz,
classical music, film and literary festivals and has a number of
cultural and historical attractions such as the Musée d'Histoire
Naturelle, Musée Dobrée, Musée Jules Verne and the Château des
Ducs de Bretagne.

Map 1.2   Second category holiday destinations

Other holiday destinations served by the airport

La Baule, Peaule, Billiers, Maine-et-loire, Pluherlin, Arzal.

Perpingnan (Pyrenees-Orientales)

Only about 40 km from the Spanish border, Perpingnan is as much Spanish as French. Tourism is a major part of its economy. Apart from the sun and sea at the Argeles-Plage and the exotic gardens of Jardin de Sant-Vicens, visitors flock to the Saint-Jean quarter, the Palais des rois de Majorque, the Cathédrale Saint-Jean and the Château de Peyrepertuse.

Other holiday destinations served by the airport
Claira, Villelongue-de-la-Salanque, Millas, Elne, St-Laurent-de-la-Salanque, Latour, Alenya, Pollestres, Bompas.

Grenoble (Isère)

For the skiing enthusiasts Grenoble is a very important destination. Located at the confluence of the Drac and Isère rivers, it is within easy reach of the finest ski resorts in the French Alps. Apart from the airport it has the further advantage of being linked to Paris by the high speed TGV network. For the less athletic visitor it has a variety of museums (Musée de L'Ancien Evêché, Musée Stendhal, Musée d'Histoire Naturelle) and a very picturesque mediaeval town centre (Place St-André). There is a jazz festival in the spring and a film festival in the summer.

Other holiday destinations served by the airport
The three main ski resorts of Isère, Savoie, and Haute-Savoie.

Brest (Finistère)

Brest is an important port for the French naval fleet and is home to the Brest Naval Training Centre. For the visitor there is no shortage of things to do: boat trips to the grottos along the Cap de la Chèvre, visits to the nature reserve (Parc Naturel Regional d'Armorique) or the Oceanopolis aquarium. There is an annual short film festival and a Tall Ships event every few years. There are Roman ruins to inspect at the nearby Village of Landevennec.

Other holiday destinations served by the airport
Crozon, Camaret-sur-Mer, Guisseny, Dirinon, Morgat, Le Conquet, Ploudalmezeau, Aberwrach, Kerlouan, Le Faou, Landunvez, Brignogan-Plage, Saint Pabu, Perros-Guirec, Henvic.

Bergerac (Dordogne)

Famous for its picturesque and quaint Old Town (*vieille ville*) Bergerac is situated on the banks of the Dordogne. Tourists can visit the nearby 16th century Recollets Convent (Cloître des Récollets) for wine tasting and concerts, check out prehistoric works of art at the Musée Nationale de Prehistoire and on the walls of a cave at the Grotte de Font de Gaume or learn something of the history of tobacco growing in Bergerac at the Musée du Tabac.

Other holiday destinations served by the airport

Issigeac, St Georges de Montclar, Mussidan, Douville, Lalinde, Maurens, Port de Couze, Sigoulès, Monpazier, Laveyssiere, Pomport, Sainte-Foy-de-Longas, Ribagnac, Plaisance, St Jean D'Eyraud, Sauveboeuf, Montpeyroux, Pressignac-Vicq, Montcaret, Prayssac.

Limoges (Haute-Vienne)

Capital of the Limousin region, Limoges is best known for its Limoges china, produced there since the late 18th century. The surrounding area also provides the finest oak wood for the barrels used in Cognac production. Tourist attractions include the stained glass windows of Eglise St-Michel des Lions, the animal park (Parc du Reynou) near the village of Solignac, the Gothic Cathedral of St-Etienne (begun in 1273) with its 62m high tower, a roman amphitheatre and the city's extensive botanical gardens.

Other holiday destinations served by the airport

Châteauroux, Chateauneuf La Forêt, Bessines Sur Gartempe, St Germain les Belles, Le Chalard, St Sornin Leulac, Eymoutiers, Saint Sulpice les Feuilles, St Léonard de Noblat, Bessines sur Gartempe.

Rennes (Ille-et-Vilaine)

Rennes is the regional capital of Brittany and is an extremely popular tourist destination. Visitors flock to the botanical gardens of the Jardin du Thabor, in the centre of the city. Every July the Tombées de la Nuit Festival transforms Rennes into a centre for music, theatre and parades (at night, of course). Other visitor attractions include the impressionist paintings of the Musée Emmanuel de la Villeon, a historical perspective on clock making at L'Atelier Musée de L'Horlogerie Ancienne and a tour of the Cathédrale Nôtre-Dame in Vitre.

Other holiday destinations served by the airport

La Bouexiere, La Meziere, La Fresnais, Saint-Cast-le-Guildo, Caden, Langon, Papillon, Pleucadeuc.

Chambery (Savoie)

Situated in the Rhône-Alpes region, South East France, Chambery has been the capital of Savoie since the 13th century. For the visitor the most striking feature of the town is the strange Fontaine des Eléphants monument, featuring four life-size elephants, commemorating some long forgotten escapade in India. Other attractions include the Château des Ducs de Savoie, home to the dukes of Savoy from 1295 to 1563, the Lac Bourget, France's largest natural lake, the Roman baths of the Thermes Nationaux and the Fine Arts Museum (Musée des Beaux-Arts) with its fine collection of Italian paintings from the Renaissance period.

Other holiday destinations served by the airport

Ski resorts of Valloire, Val Cenis, La Norma, Saint Sorlin d'Arves, Termignon, Aussois, Saint-Jean d'Arves, Orelle.

Dinard (Ille-et-Vilaine)

Located on Brittany's Côte d'Émeraude, Dinard is an extremely popular resort, offering holidaymakers a warm climate (thanks to the Gulf Stream) and the long sandy beaches of St-Enogat and Plage de l'Ecluse. Activities include kayaking, windsurfing and swimming in the Olympic sea-water pool (Piscine Olympique).

Other holiday destinations served by the airport

St Malo, Saint-Pierre-de-Plesguen, St. Enogat, Combourg, Epiniac, Manche, Cancale, Plelan-le-Petit, Matignon.

Biarritz (Pyrénées-Atlantiques)

Tourist hotspot and playground of the rich and famous, Biarritz is in the Basque region of South West France, just 18 km from Spain. People come to explore the Basque country, surf from some of the best surfing beaches available, visit the sights (Eglise Ste-Eugenie, Hôtel du Palais) or gamble in the Barrière and Bellevue casinos.

Other holiday destinations served by the airport

Guethary, Larressore, Hendaye, Anglet, Bidart, La Bastide-Clairence, St Jean de Luz-Ciboure.

Avignon (Vaucluse)

Avignon, about 80 km north of Marseille, is best known in the UK for the nursery rhyme 'Sur le pont d'Avignon'. The bridge in question is Pont Saint Bénezet, the mediaeval bridge across the Rhône, linking the old town of Avignon and Villeneuve-les-Avignon. Important tourist attractions are the Palais des Papes (home to popes in the 14th century), the 12th century cathedral (Nôtre Dame des Doms), the museum of stone carving (Musée Lapidaire) and the 14th century ramparts around the town.

Other holiday destinations served by the airport
Graveson, Cabrieres D'Avignon, Boulbon, Barthelasse, Velleron.

Montpellier (Hérault)
The country's eighth largest city and the ideal location for a Mediterranean holiday in the South of France. Not to be missed are the caves at the Grotte des Desmoiselles, the city's triumphal arch (Porte du Peyrou), day and night street entertainment in the Place de la Comédie, Montpellier Cathedral and the Amazonian greenhouse at the zoo.

Other holiday destinations served by the airport
Grabels, Juvignac, Palavas-les-Flots, St-Bauzille-de-Montmel, Beaulieu, Castries.

Table 1.4 Third category holiday destinations

Destinations	Carriers	UK/Irish airports
Carcassonne	1	8
Strasbourg	1	5
Poitiers	1	3
Beauvais	1	3
Beziers	1	2
Nimes	1	2
Rodez	1	2
Tours	1	2
Pau	1	2
Le Touquet	1	1
Angoulême	1	1
Toulon	1	1
Lorient	1	1
Caen	1	1
Deauville	1	1
Ajaccio	1	1

Map 1.3 Third category holiday destinations

PRICES AND RENTS

It is clearly essential to have an idea of prices and achievable rents before settling firmly on a location. While the rental demand may be there, the sums must add up in terms of income and outgoings – the most important of which is likely to be the cost of any mortgage taken out to finance the project.

In the UK the Royal Institution of Chartered Surveyors (RICS) produces a monthly survey of property price and rent levels throughout the UK. In France a similar report is produced by the *Fédération Nationale de l'Immobilier* (FNAIM). It is an invaluable source of information for the prospective property investor (see Appendix C).

The survey is produced quarterly and provides a breakdown of sale prices and long-term rents for apartments and houses in all the regions of the country. While regional information is of little use for our purpose, the survey also provides very specific information on the *métropoles de régions*. Most of our holiday hotspot locations are covered.

While the data on property prices is useful, however, there is a problem when it comes to rental figures. FNAIM provides figures for *long-term* rents only. There is the additional complication that the holiday season will be longer in one part of the country than another and the rents charged for the same property will vary in the low, mid- and high season. Arriving at a realistic assessment of the annual rent achievable is not a simple matter.

We have, therefore, to fall back on the only reliable source of information available on rents – the specialist holiday let websites for property owners (see Chapter 13). An examination of these shows that in the high season holiday let rents can be four times the long-term rental figure. Allowing for variations during the season, three times the long-term figure would be a realistic expectation over the season as a whole.

On this basis, drawing on the information provided by the most recent FNAIM report (prices and rents quoted per square metre), the following is a table (in euros) of prices, monthly long-term rents and holiday let rents for a 45m² apartment in our hotspot holiday let destinations covered by the report:

Table 1.5 Property prices and rents in holiday destinations

	Sale price	Long-term rent p/m	Holiday let rent p/m
Biarritz	185,985	564	1,692
Bordeaux	127,350	555	1,665
Lyon	131,580	572	1,716
Marseille	123,255	576	1,728
Montpellier	112,725	612	1,836
Nantes	114,030	542	1,626
Nice	165,150	641	1,923
Nimes	83,385	486	1,458
Paris	272,745	1,139	3,417
Pau	114,885	486	1,458
Perpignan	84,195	454	1,362
Rennes	115,785	542	1,626
Strasbourg	103,860	515	1,545
Toulon	117,450	505	1,515
Tours	94,680	514	1,542

These are, of course, average prices. There will be variations, depending on the precise district or *quartier* in which the property is located. Prices in the wider region served by the airport (see above) will be different again. There is no substitute for the expertise of the local estate agent (see Chapter 4).

2

For Long-term Letting

Renting long term is a way of life in France and there is a demand virtually everywhere for good accommodation. That is not to say, however, that there is *strong* demand everywhere and that good rents can always be achieved. There are certain towns and cities where the market is particularly active, demand is good and rents can be expected to rise in the years ahead. These are the *university* towns.

HOTSPOTS FOR LONG-TERM RENTAL

It is no coincidence that the rental market is strongest where large numbers of students need accommodation. While you may decide not to let to students (see Chapter 20), their very presence in the market substantially benefits the rental scene overall and applies upward pressure on rents. For long-term letting never be too far from a university campus.

The following are the principal university towns and cities in France:

Table 2.1   Long-term rental hotspots

Aix-en-Provence	Lille	Paris
Amiens	Limoges	Poitiers
Angers	Lyon	Reims
Besançon	Marseille	Rennes
Bordeaux	Metz	Rouen
Caen	Montpellier	Strasbourg
Clermont-Ferrand	Nancy	Toulouse
Créteil	Nantes	Tours
Dijon	Nice	Versailles
Grenoble	Orléans	

Map 2.1   Long-term rental hotspots

REFINING THE SEARCH

It is one thing to know which town or city is worth investigating for a long-term rental investment. It is another altogether to know which district or *quartier* of the town would be best.

In most cases several faculties of the university (perhaps as many as six or seven) will be located in different parts of the town. Some campuses will be bigger than others. The demand for accommodation will differ accordingly from one campus and one part of town to another.

For the non-student market good transport links and local amenities are essential. An ideal location will be close to a large campus but also within easy reach of mainline train, bus, tram or metro links and with good shopping facilities nearby.

There is only one reliable source for this information – the letting agent (*gestionnaire immobilier*). With his local knowledge and expertise he will know the best areas for the student market, the non-student market and those areas suitable for both. He will also know precisely what rents can be realistically achieved. As he will hope to get the job of managing the newly bought property he will be keen to help. It is also in his interest to point you to the very best districts as this will make the task of managing the property that much easier! Several letting agents should be approached in this way.

PRICES AND RENTS

As with a holiday letting investment, it is important to have a grasp of current property prices and rents in any chosen location.

Once again we can turn to the *Fédération Nationale de l'Immobilier* (FNAIM) (see Chapter 1 and Appendix C). Its reports provide very detailed information on prices and rents in the *métropoles de régions*, covering most of our long-term hotspot locations.

Armed with the potential sale price and annual rent it is possible to calculate the possible *gross yield* (*rendement brut*) that might be achieved for a property investment in any particular location. Comparisons can then be made with other locations. The formula is:

$$\frac{\text{Yearly rent}}{\text{Purchase price}} \times 100$$

Example

In the case, therefore, of a property bought for €155,000 and achieving an annual rent of €8900 the gross yield would be 5.7%, calculated as follows:

$$\frac{8900}{155,000} \times 100 = 5.7$$

Based on the most recent FNAIM report (prices and rents are listed per square metre) the following is a table of prices, rents and gross yields for a 45m² apartment in our hotspot locations covered by the report.

Table 2.2 Property prices, rents and yields in long-term rental locations

	Sale price	Monthly rent	Gross yield (%)
Aix-en-Provence	157,050	747	5.7
Angers	91,080	506	6.7
Bordeaux	127,350	555	5.2
Clermont- Ferrand	77,715	452	7
Dijon	97,155	503	6.2
Lyon	131,580	572	5.2
Marseille	123,255	576	5.6
Metz	86,130	434	6
Montpellier	112,725	612	6.5
Nancy	88,875	444	6
Nantes	114,030	542	5.7
Nice	165,150	641	4.7
Orléans	96,165	491	6.1
Paris	272,745	1,139	5
Reims	95,490	484	6.1
Rennes	115,785	542	5.6
Strasbourg	103,860	515	5.9
Toulouse	113,715	558	5.9
Tours	94,680	514	6.5
Versailles	224,280	846	4.5

A few points to note about these figures:

The prices and rents quoted are the average for each location. There will be variations in both for different *quartiers*. Information from local estate agents is essential to refine the search (see Chapters 4 and 20).

The yield figures quoted are *gross*, not *net*. Expenses incurred such as local taxes, agent's fees, insurance costs etc. must be factored in (i.e. deducted from the rent) to arrive at the net yield (*rendement net*).

Part Two

BUYING THE PROPERTY

3

Raising the Finance

There are essentially two ways of raising the money needed to buy a property in France. A mortgage can be raised on a property in the UK and the funds then used to buy the property for cash. Alternatively, a French mortgage can be taken out.

UK MORTGAGE

In terms of convenience a UK mortgage is clearly attractive and for this reason is frequently the first choice for many purchasers. It can take the form of a further advance on a residential or buy-to-let mortgage or a remortgage of a residential or buy-to-let mortgage. There are significant differences between these options:

Further advance

In essence this is simply a top-up to an existing mortgage. In the case of a residential mortgage the lender will need to establish that there is sufficient equity in the property and that the income of the borrower can meet the additional cost. In the case of the buy-to-let mortgage the criteria are different. Here the lender will consider whether the current loan-to-value is low enough to accommodate the further advance (or *drawdown* as it is commonly called) and whether the rental income on the buy-to-let will exceed the new monthly payments by the required amount. In neither case will the potential income from the French property be taken into account.

The attraction of a further advance or drawdown is the relatively low cost and minimal paperwork involved. In the worst case scenario the lender will require a valuation and a valuation fee. In some cases, where the equity in the property is obviously substantial, a valuation may not even be required. There is also the very clear advantage of being able to draw on the funds only when they are required, thus avoiding the extra cost involved until absolutely necessary.

Remortgage

While the same lending criteria are likely to be applicable, a remortgage involves a change of lender. This would normally be considered only if the current lender is proving difficult and unaccommodating or there is a much more attractive interest rate available elsewhere. The reason for this is the cost and time involved. Moving from one lender to another is an expensive and time-consuming business. A new mortgage application has to be submitted to the new lender. A valuation will always be required and legal costs incurred. A redemption penalty may be imposed by the existing lender. The new lender will also undertake all the usual credit checks and background enquiries applicable to a new mortgage application. Finally, in the case of a remortgage, the full amount will normally be drawn when the application has been accepted. It may not, however, be needed for some time. If the purchase falls through it may be a very long time before it is called upon. In the meantime it has to be paid for.

PROS AND CONS OF UK FINANCE

All vendors love a cash buyer! By raising the purchase price in this way the buyer starts with a clear advantage. Secondly, as the funds are already available, the transaction can be completed that much more quickly. There are, however, some significant drawbacks to consider:

- If the cash is raised through a remortgage (see above) the cost of servicing the loan will be incurred immediately, perhaps long before it is used to purchase a property.

- Interest rates in the UK are usually higher than in the eurozone. A French mortgage will normally be cheaper.

- Currency fluctuations are an obvious source of uncertainty. Pounds have to be converted to euros when transferred to France for the purchase. If the pound suddenly falls in value against the euro, more pounds will be needed to complete the sale. Suddenly the price of the French property has gone up. When it comes to selling the property the currency situation will again be a factor.

- Interest paid on a French mortgage can be used to set against French tax. Interest on a UK loan cannot be used this way in France.

Tips

Make sure the funds are actually in place before signing a compromis de vente (see Chapter 6) and committing to the purchase. There is no clause suspensive (see Chapter 6) in a French contract that allows a purchaser to pull out if a UK mortgage fails to materialise. This safeguard is only available for a French mortgage. As far as the vendor is concerned you are buying sans crédit (no mortgage required).

Don't automatically use your own bank to convert and transfer the funds abroad. Foreign exchange brokers invariably offer a better exchange rate for large sum transactions. See Appendix C.

If the exchange rate is currently very favourable you can lock into this rate by taking out a 'forward contract' for a specified time (e.g. three months). This means that for this period you are guaranteed a fixed exchange rate, whatever happens to the value of the pound.

FRENCH MORTGAGE (*prêt immobilier*)

Little has changed over the years in the French mortgage market. To describe it as traditional would be a serious understatement. This has, however, helped to produce a relatively stable housing market, largely protected from the boom and bust volatility brought about by the reckless lending of pre credit-crunch Britain.

Mortgages available

There are two types of mortgage available in France – the *Privilège de Prêteur de Deniers* and *Hypothèque Conventionnelle*.

A distinction is drawn between purchasing a property already built and buying one under construction (off plan). In the first case the mortgage taken out is called a *Privilège de Prêteur de Deniers* and constitutes a first charge on the property. In the second case a conventional mortgage has to be used – *Hypothèque Conventionnelle*. This also has to be used if a mortgage already exists on the property and the owner wishes to obtain a further advance from the lender.

The distinction between the two is significant as the costs involved differ considerably. See below.

The lenders

Given the long tradition of foreigners buying in France, there is no shortage of eager and willing mortgage lenders. In most cases there are dedicated websites in English and English-speaking advisors at the end of the phone line. The following are the principal players in the market for overseas buyers:

- Barclays

- BNP PARIBAS

- *Crédit Foncier*

- *Crédit Lyonnais*

- CIC

- *Crédit Agricole*

- HSBC

For contact details, see Appendix C.

French mortgage brokers (*courtiers en prêt*)

It is certainly tempting to hand the whole business over to a broker in France (a simple Google search for 'French mortgage broker' will provide an ample selection to choose from). At first glance there would seem to be compelling reasons to do so:

- If language is a problem there is no shortage of English-speaking brokers in the French market.

- By definition, a good broker knows the market and can find the best deal to suit his client, saving a great deal of time and effort.

- He can also negotiate preferential terms on rates or fees.

- It is also the case (as in the UK) that brokers sometimes have access to more favourable products not available direct from the lenders.

- In addition to mortgage products the broker will also know the insurance market and will be able to source the right policy at the right price for the life cover and buildings cover required.

So what, you might ask, is the downside? Considerable care needs to be taken in the choice of mortgage broker in France.

First, there is the question of fees. As in the UK, some brokers charge fees (*frais de courtier*) some don't. As in the UK there is absolutely no reason to choose a broker who charges the client a fee. The reason is simply that the lender, in all cases, pays the broker a fee (typically 1%) for the business he introduces, regardless of whether he is paid by the client or not. If the client is also charged then the broker has been paid twice and the client is seriously out of pocket.

It is illegal in France for a broker to ask for any payment, however small (including his own fee or the lender's arrangement fee), before the mortgage has been agreed and the funds released (article L321-2 of the *Code de la Consommation* 2001). That is not to say that a broker will not make such a demand, especially when the client is a foreigner.

The next issue is the status of the broker. Is he independent (i.e. able to trawl the whole marketplace for a mortgage) or is he limited to a selected (and limited) number of lenders? The corresponding terms in the UK are 'whole of market' and 'panel'.

Finally, a broker can, in fact, slow things down considerably if he is very busy, understaffed or simply not very good. Every communication between lender and client must be channelled through him.

UK-based brokers

There are a few brokers in the UK who specialise in sourcing overseas mortgages (see Appendix C). The same caveats as those outlined above (fees, independence etc.) apply when choosing one.

Loan-to-value

As a general rule French lenders are a good deal more cautious than their British counterparts and a substantial deposit is a normal requirement. For the non-resident buyer 70–80% of the purchase price is as much as can normally be expected. It is worth noting here that lenders will generally include in this the fee charged by the estate agent (*agent immobilier*) as this is included in the price. The *notaire*'s fees, however, will not be advanced by the lender.

Mortgage products

Considering their generally conservative approach to mortgages, French lenders offer a surprising degree of flexibility in their product range:

Fixed rate mortgages (*prêts à taux fixe*)

These are widely available in France but, unlike their UK equivalent, are generally for the full term of the mortgage (instead of the typical two or three-year offering in Britain). The borrower, therefore, has the security of knowing his exact monthly payments for the entire duration of the loan – perhaps 20 years. As with fixed rates in the UK there is a redemption charge if the loan is repaid before the fixed term expires. In France, however, this cannot exceed 3% of the amount redeemed. In the UK lenders can charge what they like. Fixed rate interest rates are generally higher than variable rates.

Variable rate mortgages (*prêts à taux revisable*)

In France these are unlike anything available in the UK. They are frequently offered with an initial *fixed* rate for three months or a year, after which the rate is reviewed according to the lender's margin above the prevailing EURIBOR rate (the rate at which European banks lend to each other) and set for another period of three months or a year. At any time the borrower can switch to a fixed rate mortgage. In many cases the lender will also *cap* any future increases (e.g. limiting any increase to 2% above the initial rate). It is even possible for monthly payments to remain unchanged from year to year, despite increases in interest rates (the term of the mortgage is adjusted instead). About the only thing in common with the UK version of the variable rate mortgage is the absence of an early redemption penalty. Variable interest rates are always lower than fixed.

Repayment options

As in the UK both *'capital and interest'* and *'interest only'* options are available. In the case of the capital and interest mortgage (*prêt classique* or *prêt amortisable*) the loan is repaid over the term of the mortgage. With an interest only mortgage (*prêt in fine*) no capital is repaid and monthly payments cover the interest only (for that reason interest only mortgages are considerably cheaper to service). The capital is paid in a lump sum at the end of the mortgage term.

Traditionally French lenders have favoured the capital and interest system (usually called 'repayment' in the UK) and have only recently come to accept 'interest only' as a viable option. For that reason the borrower looking for an interest only mortgage may come across some unexpected variations:

■ Some lenders will consider this type of mortgage only if the borrower can prove he already has substantial savings and assets from which he can repay the capital when the time comes. In other words, only the rich need apply.

■ Others will require a savings vehicle (*contrat d'épargne*) to be put in place alongside the mortgage, with the capital to be paid from this when the mortgage comes to an end. In this case, however, the advantage of the lower monthly cost associated with the interest only mortgage is reduced or eliminated as contributions have to be made to the savings vehicle.

■ A further variation is a hybrid mortgage – a combination of
   interest only and repayment. In this case the borrower is
   effectively given a capital repayment holiday for the early part
   of the mortgage (typically five to ten years), during which he
   will make interest payments only. Capital payments, however,
   will be required during the remaining years of the mortgage.
   While this has clear benefits in the interest only period it can
   cause major problems later on. The whole of the outstanding
   capital has to be repaid over a very short period, making for
   greatly increased monthly payments.

Maximum borrowing

Perhaps the most striking aspect of the French mortgage system
(from a UK borrower's perspective) is the very traditional
calculation of affordability applied by French lenders. There is,
for example, no question of a self-certfication mortgage (where
the borrower simply declares his income and provides no proof
of it). Nor do the French work on a multiple-of-income calculation
(e.g. 3.5 × single gross income or 2.75 × joint, as is common in
the UK).

Instead, they start with the borrower's *current gross monthly
income* (some lenders insist on the *net* figure). Only 33% of this
income can be used to service both the new mortgage and life cover
premiums (see below) *and* all existing financial commitments,
such as credit card payments, personal loan payments, other
mortgage payments, maintenance payments, rent payments
on another property etc. For joint applications the income and
liabilities of both applicants are taken into account).

Example

Monthly income	4,000
33% × income	1,320
Financial commitments	800

Available to cover new mortgage 520 (1,320 – 800)

While this formula is standard throughout the mortgage market, it is not necessarily set in stone. Lenders can show some flexibility in their underwriting when dealing, for example, with high net-worth applicants.

Buy-to-let mortgage

Needless to say, such a strict set of criteria would rule out many property investors who are looking to the future rental income (rather than their own surplus income) to fund the purchase. The French do, in fact, have a buy-to-let mortgage market but it differs significantly from its UK equivalent.

In the UK lenders look to the potential rental income to cover the mortgage outgoings on the new property. As a general rule the income should be 125% or 130% of the monthly mortgage interest payments. It is not normally necessary to take into account the applicant's personal income and outgoings and proof of these is not generally required. French buy-to-let mortgages, however, are *full status*. In other words, French lenders require full documentation regarding the applicant's personal income and outgoings even though the future rental income is intended to fund the mortgage.

As for the rental income itself, lenders in France can take differing views. Some will not take it into account at all. They expect the new mortgage to be funded under the '33% gross income rule', disregarding any rental income generated. This is clearly of little use to an investor. Others will take the potential rental income into account, but not all of it. The maximum is normally 80%. Where the rent is taken into account in this way the lender will add it to the borrower's other income before applying the '33% gross income rule'. For most buy-to-let purchasers this formula is essential.

All lenders expect to be told at the application stage if the property is to be let out.

Finance for leaseback, long-term and holiday lets

Mortgage lenders do not treat all forms of buy-to-let investment in the same way and some important distinctions need to be drawn.

A leaseback mortgage is a specialist area, involving staged drawdown of mortgage funds as the building work proceeds. The borrower pays interest only on the amount advanced. Some lenders will allow this interest to be deferred for up to two years (to be added later to the mortgage payments).

Not all lenders are in this market. For those who are, however, the leaseback formula has clear attractions. The rent, after all, is guaranteed whether the property is let or not. For this reason the lender will have few qualms about taking the rent into account and setting it against the mortgage payments, before calling on the '33% gross income' rule (see above). It is also possible that a higher loan-to-value may be permitted than would otherwise be the case and a longer mortgage term than usual can be more easily negotiated. On the downside, however, is the smaller pool of lenders from which a borrower can choose. Indeed, in many cases, the developer will already have an arrangement with a mortgage lender and will strongly promote his services to any potential purchaser. A choice of one!

The traditional long-term let (three-year lease) is acceptable to most lenders though not all will take the potential rent into account when calculating the mortgage they are prepared to offer. A letting agent's valuation and an agreement with an agent to manage the property could prove persuasive in this regard. Some lenders may insist that a letting agent manage the property and will want to see a signed agency agreement to that effect.

The holiday let scene is more problematic. Few lenders will consider seasonal letting as a secure source of income and it will be difficult to find any willing to take such potential income into account when making a mortgage offer.

Mortgage fees

As in the UK, taking out a mortgage in France is an expensive business. Most lenders charge an arrangement fee (*frais de dossier*) of between 0.5% and 1% of the amount borrowed, with a minimum of €700 and a maximum of €1,500 usually stipulated. This compares favourably with UK lenders who set no upper limit. In the UK, however, it is unlikely that the borrower will have to find the fee upfront. It is routinely added to the mortgage (an additional source of revenue for the lender, as interest will be paid on it for the duration of the mortgage!). In France the fee is paid separately and must be found from the borrower's own resources.

There is a fee in France for registering a standard mortgage (*hypothèque conventionnelle*) at the land registry office (*bureau des hypothèques*). This can be up to 2% of the loan. With the alternative *Privilège de Prêteur de Deniers* (see above) which also has to be registered, the cost is lower as no tax or stamp duty (*taxe de publicité foncière*) is payable. The cost in this case is between 1% and 1.5% of the loan amount.

A peculiarity of the French system is the tax levied by the government where a certificate is required to show that the mortgage has been redeemed before the end of the term. This is most likely to occur when the property is being sold. The new purchaser requires evidence that the mortgage has been cleared. This declaration of mortgage release (*mainlevée*) must be obtained through a *notaire* and the bill (typically 0.5%) is met by the borrower. Even when the mortgage has run to term there is a risk of incurring this cost. The owner must keep the property for one year after the mortgage has been redeemed before he can obtain the *mainlevée* for nothing!

Redemption penalties (*pénalités de remboursement anticipé*)

As with UK mortgages a penalty can be imposed for the early redemption of a French mortgage. This applies only in the case of fixed rate mortgages and is typically six months' interest, capped at 3% of the amount outstanding. This compares favourably with the UK equivalent where there is no upper limit on the penalty that can be charged (5% is not uncommon). Variable rate mortgages do not incur a charge.

If the redemption is made following the sale of the property the penalty cannot be imposed if the sale was due to redundancy, job relocation or death. In the UK there are no exemptions of this sort.

Mortgage term

French mortgage terms are shorter than in the UK, with a range of five to 20 years being the norm. Mortgages of 25 or 30 years are unusual. The upper-age limit on completion is 70, the maximum expiry age for life insurance policies (see below).

Life insurance (*assurance décès*)

Taking out life cover with a new mortgage is a prudent course of action and is routinely available, as an option, in the UK. In France, however, it is not an option. It is *mandatory*. Just as the lender needs to be convinced that the borrower can afford the mortgage in the first place, he also needs to know that it will be redeemed entirely on death, leaving no financial headaches for next-of-kin. The lender will take a legal charge on the policy. No life cover, no mortgage!

The type of cover depends on the method of repayment. If the mortgage is capital and interest the policy will be on a *reducing cover* basis. This means that the sum assured (the amount paid on death) will reduce as the mortgage capital is repaid. This is the cheapest form of cover available. If the mortgage taken out is interest only, however, the capital is not repaid at all until the end of the mortgage term. The life cover required in this case must be *level term assurance*. The sum assured remains the same throughout the term because the entire capital would need to be repaid whenever death occurs. The cost of this type of insurance is considerably higher as the risk to the insurer remains constant throughout the term. Whichever policy is used, the term of the cover must correspond to the term of the mortgage. A 20-year mortgage will require a 20-year policy.

Many lenders go further and require disability or sickness cover (*assurance décès-invalidité*) in addition to the life cover. A policy that incorporates this would clear the mortgage on death or pay the mortgage payments in the event of temporary illness (*garantie incapacité temporaire de travail*) or long-term illness (*garantie invalidité permanente totale*) with payments normally commencing three months after onset of the illness. Applicants who have retired or reached retirement age will not qualify for this cover (life cover only can be provided).

In the case of a joint application (required for a joint mortgage) the level of cover (the 'sum assured') can be allocated in accordance with the income of the applicants. For a mortgage of €100,000, for example, one applicant could be covered for €60,000 and the other for €40,000. Alternatively they could choose to be each covered for €100,000, though the premiums in this case would be higher.

While individual policies are the norm in the UK many French banks have an arrangement with an insurance company to provide a group policy (*assurance groupe*). In this case every new borrower is covered by the same terms and conditions of the group plan. The lender must explain in detail what these terms are and highlight any special clauses which could adversely affect the applicant. The borrower can choose to go elsewhere to buy a policy (*contrat d'assurances externe*) with lower premiums or better terms. This may be particularly advantageous for the young applicant in good health.

Depending on the type of policy and age of the applicant premiums can be anywhere between 0.18% and 0.7% of the sum borrowed.

Whichever type of policy is used it will need to be underwritten in the normal way. An application form (*formulaire d'assurance*) is completed along with a health questionnaire (*questionnaire de santé*) and the insurance company's underwriters will assess the risk. Care should be taken to complete the questionnaire fully and truthfully as claims can be rejected in cases of non-disclosure. The insurance application is strictly confidential and the applicant can choose to send it back directly to the insurer instead of via the lender.

A medical examination may be required (depending on the age and health of the applicant). This can be arranged in the UK, with the insurance company meeting the cost. The monthly premiums (*primes d'assurances*) for the policy will either be as originally quoted or given a 'loading' (*surprime*) if the underwriters have reservations about the details on the application form or the results of the medical. It is also possible that the underwriters will want to exclude certain risks (e.g. cancer or heart disease) from cover and will apply an exclusion (*exclusion médicale*) to that effect. In rare cases they may refuse cover altogether. As life cover is essential for a mortgage this would clearly cause problems for a minority of people.

On 6 January 2007 the '*Convention AERAS*' (*S'Assurer et Emprunter avec un Risque Aggravé de Santé*) was established to provide cover for high-risk individuals (see Appendix C). To qualify, the applicant must be no older than 70 at the end of the mortgage term and the amount borrowed must not exceed €300,000. A health questionnaire has to be completed in the usual way. There is an appeals procedure if the applicant is unhappy with the outcome (see Appendix C).

It is worth noting that the cost of the policy (the monthly premiums) must be covered by the '33% gross income' rule (see above). Most lenders also insist that the policy be put in place once it is underwritten, even if the mortgage has not yet been finalised. In the case of a leaseback purchase (where the mortgage is paid in stages over many months as the work proceeds) the monthly premiums will be an ongoing expense for some considerable time before the mortgage is finalised and the property purchased.

Lenders always assume that the borrower will use the policy they offer and frequently supply the life policy form at the same time as the application form for the mortgage itself. The reason for this is that they are paid commission by the underwriting insurance company for each policy sold (just as UK banks are) and do not want to encourage the borrower to go elsewhere. The borrower, however, is not obliged to accept the lender's insurance and can opt to go elsewhere to get comparable cover.

When it comes to using a policy already held by the borrower, lenders may be prepared to accept such a policy if it meets all the requirements of the new mortgage. It must not only fit the term of the mortgage and the amount borrowed, it must also be sufficiently adjustable to accommodate possible changes to the mortgage in the future. French mortgages are a good deal more flexible than their UK counterparts, allowing, for example, an increase or reduction in the term and a switch from repayment to interest only or vice versa. Few UK life policies can be adjusted in this way. There is the further complication of a policy denominated in sterling, instead of euros. To allow for future exchange rate fluctuations the French lender may insist on a higher sum assured than is strictly necessary to cover the mortgage at the time it is taken out.

FRENCH MORTGAGE PROCESS

For the mortgage applicant accustomed to the UK system the application process in France can seem tortuous. French lenders require everything.

Documentation

It goes without saying that there is a mortgage application form (*formulaire de demande de prêt*) to be completed. But this is just the beginning. To be returned with this is the life policy application form (see above) and a bewildering array of supporting documents:

Commitment to buy

It would seem fairly obvious that a mortgage applicant must be serious about buying the property. The French lender, however, requires proof. A copy of the *compromis de vente* or, in the case of an off-plan purchase, the *contrat de réservation* (see Chapter 8) must be provided.

Proof of income

For an employee the last three months' pay slips and the most recent P60 will be required. The lender may also ask for a reference from the applicant's employer confirming salary, position held in the company and length of service. For the self-employed applicant the lender needs confirmation of his net income (i.e. income after expenses but before tax). To this end two or three years' audited accounts and tax returns will be expected. A letter from his accountant may also be called for. In all cases original documents only will be accepted.

Proof of outgoings

As French lenders work on a strict affordability basis (see above) they will want full details of current financial commitments. If the applicant is renting a property the tenancy agreement will need to be provided. In the case of personal loans and credit cards, loan agreements and recent statements will be required. If there is an existing mortgage in place the last mortgage statement will be required together with confirmation from the lender that the mortgage has been paid to date. Where there are any other regular financial commitments the relevant documents for these will be need to be produced. Finally, The last three months' bank statements must be provided. It will be expected that these will show all the monthly debits for the outgoings referred to.

Proof of deposit

While lenders in the UK tend to accept the borrower's word for the existence of the deposit (in the knowledge that it will probably be provided by friends or relatives when the time comes), French lenders require proof that it is available *right now*. To this end, a bank statement or savings deposit statement showing the existence of the necessary funds will have to be provided.

Proof of ID and address

The lender will want to know who you are, when you were born, who you are married to and where you live. Proof of all this is required. Be prepared, therefore, to provide a birth certificate, marriage certificate, passport and, for proof of your address, some recent utility bills.

And so on . . .

It may not end there! Be prepared for supplementary questions.

Valuation

If all goes well the lender will announce that a valuation will be carried out. This is not a survey and it will not cover the structural condition of the building. It is broadly similar to the valuation carried out by UK lenders. The purpose is simply to check that the price offered is in line with current market conditions. The cost of this valuation is normally covered by the rather generous arrangement fee charged by the lender. Some lenders, however, may charge separately for this (typically €500).

Mortgage offer

When a satisfactory valuation has been obtained and the life insurance policy has been underwritten a preliminary offer (*offre préalable d'un crédit immobilier*) will be issued. This must be sent by recorded post (with a copy going to the *notaire*) and must not be signed and returned until ten days have elapsed from the date of receipt (the statutory cooling-off period). In other words the earliest day it can be signed by the applicant is 11 days after receipt. The offer is valid for a minimum of 30 days (maximum four months) and must be returned within the specified time.

There are strict legal obligations on the lender (*Loi Scrivener*) with regards to the content of the offer letter. Certain details must be included:

(a) Name and address of the borrower.

(b) Name and address of the lender.

(c) A reminder of the obligatory cooling-off period.

(d) The amount to be borrowed, the purpose of the loan, the interest rate, method of repayment, penalties for early redemption, details of the insurance cover that will be required, the term of the mortgage and the date funds will be available.

(e) In addition to the headline interest rate the offer must state the overall total rate or 'Global Effective Rate' applicable (*le taux effectif global du prêt or TEG*). This is much the same as the Annual Equivalent Rate (AER) in the UK and will take into account other costs such as arrangement fees, insurance premiums etc. As in the UK it is intended to make it easier for borrowers to compare 'real' interest rates among lenders.

(f) The total cost of the borrowing (i.e. capital and interest) over the full term of the mortgage.

(g) A schedule of repayments over the term. This must show separate entries for capital and interest.

Bank account and direct debit

Payments to the lender are made by direct debit on a French bank account. It will be necessary to open an account, if you haven't already done so (see Chapter 11), and complete the direct debit mandate. Some lenders require that you open a bank account with them for this purpose. This will have been made clear at the application stage.

Life policy and arrangement fee

The life insurance policy will be put on risk as soon as the mortgage offer letter is returned (although it may be some time before the mortgage itself starts). The premiums, like the mortgage payments, will be paid by direct debit. The arrangement fee will normally be taken by direct debit when the first mortgage payment is made. Some lenders. However, may require this to be paid when the offer letter is returned.

Transfer of funds

The borrower now transfers the deposit to the *notaire* and the lender transfers the mortgage funds. The *notaire* is now in a position to complete the transaction.

Timescale

Anything from six to 12 weeks from application to transfer of funds.

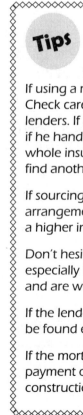

Tips

If using a mortgage broker ask for written terms of business. Check carefully if the broker is independent and can deal with all lenders. If he charges fees find a broker who doesn't. Check also if he handles insurance products and can source these from the whole insurance market. If any payment is required in advance find another broker.

If sourcing a mortgage directly from lenders compare both arrangement fees and interest rates. A low arrangement fee with a higher interest rate may be poor value in the long term.

Don't hesitate to negotiate with lenders both on fees and rates, especially if you are prepared to open a bank account with them and are willing to take their insurance products.

If the lender offers only group life cover check if better terms can be found elsewhere with an individual policy.

If the mortgage is for an off-plan purchase check whether payment of interest on the funds advanced during the construction can be deferred until the project is complete.

PROS AND CONS OF A FRENCH MORTGAGE

Among the attractions of a French mortgage are the following:

- Interest rates in France have historically been lower than in the UK.

- French mortgage products are a great deal more flexible than those offered by UK lenders.

- The very tight affordability rules in France reduces the risk that the borrower will come unstuck later on in the mortgage.

- The interest paid on a French mortgage can be set against rental income in France for tax purposes (see Chapter 21). Any potential inheritance tax or wealth tax liability in France is reduced or avoided altogether while there is a French mortgage on a property. For tax purposes the value of the property is reduced by the outstanding mortgage liability (see Chapters 24 and 25).

- Taking on a mortgage necessarily entails risk. The property could be repossessed if the borrower defaults. In the case of a French mortgage this risk is solely on the French property. If the mortgage is raised on a property in the UK (perhaps on the borrower's principal residence) it is that property which is at risk.

Against these advantages should be set the following:

- Exchange rate fluctuations could pose a serious hazard if the mortgage is funded by income generated in the UK. If sterling falls in value the cost of servicing the euro mortgage will rise.

One option is to consider funding the purchase through a combination of a UK and a French mortgage.

- Mortgage terms are shorter in France, with 15 years being the most common. A 25-year term (standard in the UK) may be difficult to find.

- An interest only mortgage which is not linked to a savings scheme may also be difficult to source.

- It may not be possible to meet the very strict affordability criteria French lenders impose.

4

Finding the Property

As in the UK most property in France is bought and sold through local estate agents and they are the most likely source of a suitable investment property. A Google search will locate those in the area of your choice. Many, with an eye to foreign buyers, have websites in English. An alternative approach is to hand the whole business over to a 'property finder'. A search on the web for 'property finder France' or for a precise location such as 'property finder Paris' will provide a wide choice of French and bi-lingual finders competing for your business.

ESTATE AGENTS (*agences immobilières*)

Since January 1970 estate agents have been legally regulated by the *Loi Hoguet* which lays down a number of strict requirements for the profession. They are:

1. Under article 3 no agent can trade without a licence or *carte professionnelle*. This guarantees that the agent is properly qualified, has adequate financial guarantees to safeguard any deposits, has an appropriate level of indemnity insurance and has not been disqualified from acting as an estate agent. The *carte* must be renewed annually. There are three kinds issued – *carte 'T'* (*transactions sur immeubles et fonds de commerce*) for property sales, *carte 'G'* (*gestion immobilière*) for letting

and managing rented properties and a *carte* exclusively for *marchands de liste de location* (agents who simply provide lists of property to let). An application for a *carte professionnelle* must be made to the local *préfecture* (in the case of Paris, to the *Préfet de Police*).

2. Reasons for disqualification include a conviction for any crime within the last ten years or a prison sentence for a wide range of offences including fraud, receiving stolen goods, money laundering, drug trafficking and many others.

3. An agent must have passed the *baccalauréat* (or equivalent) and have undertaken a further three years of study in law, economics or business. Alternatively, there are various diploma courses specific to the profession which will provide acceptable qualifications. In the absence of any formal qualifications, however, ten years' professional experience may be accepted, reduced to three years if the applicant has passed the *baccalauréat* or equivalent.

Infringement of the *Loi Hoguet* is a serious matter. The penalty is a fine or imprisonment.

Professional bodies

Apart from the strict entry requirements to the profession, estate agents will be expected to belong to one of the estate agents' professional bodies – *Fédération Nationale de l'Immobilier* (FNAIM) or *Professionnels Immobiliers* (SNPI). See Appendix C.

These organisations expect their members to adhere to a strict professional code of conduct (*code d'éthique et de déontologie*), to act legally at all times, to keep abreast of changes in the regulatory regime affecting the profession and to maintain adequate indemnity insurance (*assurance en responsabilité civile professionnelle*) at all times. They also expect their members to be completely open and transparent about their qualifications, the services offered and the fees charged.

Membership of a professional body is displayed prominently (and proudly) on the agent's letterheads and website.

Fees (*honoraires*)

In the UK the agent's fee is always paid by the vendor who, after all, instructs him to sell the property. In France it can be the vendor (*vendeur*) or the purchaser (*acquéreur*) who pays the fee, though it is more usual for the vendor to do so. In either case the potential purchaser must be made fully aware of the situation. Where the vendor is responsible the asking price of the property includes the agent's commission (*commission comprise* or C/C). If the purchaser is expected to pay the fee the sale price quoted must be broken down to the component parts – the net price (i.e. *prix net*) and the commission. This will be made clear in both the preliminary contract and the final contract. When this happens the price quoted at the point of sale is often referred to as *net vendeur*. In other words, this is what the vendor will receive (the purchaser will pay commission on top).

When it comes to the level of fees charged estate agents in France have no choice but to be fully transparent. The scale of fees (*barème*) must be displayed in the window and the reception area of the agency. Unlike the *notaire*'s fees which are fixed by law, there is no restriction on what estate agents can charge. In practice the range is generally between 4% and 8%, inclusive of VAT or *TVA* (*toutes taxes comprises* or *TTC*), depending on the price of the property. The cheaper the property the higher the fee and vice versa.

Under article 6 of the *Loi Hoguet* no payment of any kind can be made before the final contract is signed.

Tips

Check that the agent has the appropriate carte professionnelle (T) entitling him to handle property sales. This will be found on all agency literature and will typically read: 'Carte professionnelle no. . . . (T) delivrée par la Préfecture . . .'

Check that the agent belongs to a professional body. This will also be prominently displayed along with the level of financial guarantee held by the agency e.g. 'Garantie FNAIM 300 000€'.

Check whether the prices quoted are commission comprise (C/C) or whether you are expected to pay the agent's fees.

Don't be afraid to negotiate. Like their UK counterparts French estate agents will expect you to haggle. If you are not taking out a French mortgage for the purchase you are, as far as the vendor is concerned, a 'cash buyer' and are therefore in a very strong position.

THE PROPERTY FINDER (*chasseur immobilier*)

For many people the task of locating and buying a property abroad can seem too difficult and time consuming to undertake. Apart from all the usual problems associated with any property purchase there are the additional complications of a foreign language, a strange legal system, a different culture and little or no knowledge of local conditions. Enter the property finder.

The traditional property finder was typically someone who had successfully bought a property abroad and who offered his help and advice (for a fee) to others wishing to do the same. He would locate suitable properties, arrange visits, advise on the buying process etc. The arrangement was largely informal and seemed to escape the plethora of regulations and restrictions that estate agents were subjected to. All this has changed.

Nothing in France remains unregulated for long! It is now generally accepted that the *Loi Hoguet* (see above) which regulates estate agents can also apply to the property finder (*chasseur immobillier*). If the finder sources his properties through estate agents and shares their commission he will be covered by the law. Likewise if he negotiates the price on behalf of the buyer or is in any way involved in the legal process leading to the sale he is caught by article 1 of the law. Only if his function is limited to sourcing suitable properties, for which he is paid solely and exclusively by the buyer, is he free of the act. Given these restrictions (and the severe penalties for infringing the law) most *chasseurs immobiliers* have decided to take no risks. They now comply with the *Loi Hoguet*. For that reason they have a *carte professionnelle* just like an estate agent and, like an estate agent, in compliance with the law, receive no remuneration at all until the sale is complete.

Professional bodies

To highlight further the arrival of the property finder as a mainstream profession, two professional bodies have recently been set up to oversee his activities. They are *Fédération Nationale des Chasseurs Immobiliers* (FNCI) and *La Fédération Française des Chasseurs Immobiliers* (FFCI). See Appendix C.

Like the equivalent organisations for estate agents they boast a strict code of professional ethics (*charte de déontologie des chasseurs immobiliers*). Members are required to carry the appropriate *carte professionnelle* and must undertake to accept no payment until the purchase is complete. They must be completely open about the fees they charge and keep accurate records of the work they do and the time they spend on the clients' behalf. They must keep their clients informed and fully advised at all times. They must always respect their clients' confidentiality. Lastly, they must draw up a suitable agreement with their clients (see below) and respect the terms of that agreement.

Services offered

The property finder claims to differ fundamentally from the estate agent in that he works exclusively for the *purchaser* – unlike the estate agent who is instructed by and works solely for the vendor. In addition, the *chasseur immobilier* will offer the following:

1. A highly personal and tailor-made (*sur-mesure*) service. Only after an in-depth analysis of his client's requirements (often carried out in the client's own home or place of work) will he begin his search. Only properties fitting his client's precise requirements (type of property, budget, location etc.) will be presented for consideration, thus saving a great deal of time.

2. A choice of properties from a variety of sources – local estate agents, *notaires* (many of whom sell properties) and private vendors. All will be presented with photos and full specifications. The client can also expect information not normally provided by an estate agent such as the level of local taxes or the rules of the *copropriété* (see Chapter 7) if the property in question is an apartment. When a property is selected he will negotiate on price.

3. Visits arranged to view properties. Hotel accommodation booked if necessary.

4. Advice on the legal process, an introduction to an English speaking *notaire* and attendance at the contract signing. If the client wishes to leave all this to the finder he can sign the appropriate power of attorney (*procuration*) and let the finder conclude the legal formalities on his behalf.

Fees (*honoraires*)

As might be expected, all this comes at a price. Unlike the estate agent who has just one task to perform (finding a buyer) the property finder could be involved in a number of time-consuming activities apart from the actual sourcing of a suitable property. For this reason the likely cost of the service is not normally made clear until an initial analysis of the client's needs has been made. As a general rule, however, expect to pay between 2.5% and 5% of the purchase price.

The agreement (*mandat de recherche*)

While the estate agent has a formal agreement with the vendor (*mandat de vente*) the property finder will not embark on his task without a similar agreement with his client (*mandat de recherche*). The purchaser must authorise him in writing to search for suitable properties. Although there is no set format for a *mandat de recherche* the following clauses at least can be expected:

■ The term of the agreement. The property finder cannot expect an open-ended instruction to find a property, regardless of how long it might take to achieve this. A term of three months is standard. An option to renew for a further three months is also standard.

■ The finder undertakes to search for properties according to the precise requirements of the purchaser.

- The client undertakes not to instruct another property finder or to buy direct from the vendor during the term of the agreement. In other words, the client has a sole agency agreement with the finder.

- The finder may specify a minimum number of properties to be sourced during the term of the agreement. He may also set out the way the properties will be presented to the client.

- The property finder undertakes to respect his client's confidentiality.

- The bill the client can expect to receive for the work undertaken.

Tips

Given the cost, consider carefully whether this level of service is really needed. There is normally no cost involved in using an estate agent.

Check the property finder's status. If a full service is offered then he should have a carte professionnelle and belong to one of the professional bodies.

Just as a vendor will compare the fees charged by estate agents a purchaser should do likewise when choosing a property finder. It is a competitive business.

On no account pay anything unless and until the purchase is complete.

5

French Inheritance Law

It may seem strange to consider the issue of passing on a property to your heirs before you have even bought it! But in France this is essential. *How* you buy a property in France determines what happens to it on your death. The issue is particularly important for two people buying jointly.

In the UK, when property is bought jointly, it can be held in one of two ways – as *joint tenants* or *tenants in common* (the word 'tenants' here does not have its usual meaning). In the first case the property is owned jointly and, on the first death, passes automatically to the survivor. In the case of tenancy in common, however, each owns his own portion of the property (normally a 50/50 split but it could be any split desired). On the first death, in this case, what happens to the deceased's share will depend on the terms of his will. He could leave it to his spouse, his children or the cats' home. If there is a will the terms of the will must be honoured. If he dies without making a will the rules of intestacy will decide who benefits and in what proportion (spouse, children, brothers, sisters, parents, uncles, aunts).

In France the position appears, at first glance, to be similar. There is a 'joint tenancy' style system where the property passes on death to the survivor (*en tontine*). This is rare and is open to challenge by children and other relatives who may claim they have been disinherited (see below). There is also a 'tenancy in common' arrangement where each holds his own separate share of the property (*en indivision*). This is the norm and will automatically apply unless the *notaire* is told otherwise. He won't ask! Despite these similarities, however, the situation is far from simple. Welcome to the complex world of French inheritance law.

In France it is not legally possible to disinherit children, parents or other members of the immediate family. In this respect the law takes precedence over the terms of a will. Where there are children a surviving spouse is not entitled to the whole estate even if that is the wish of the deceased, as expressed in his will. A specified proportion of the deceased's estate (*réserve légale*) must go to the children. If there is just one child he will receive half. Two children would receive one third each. If there are three or more children they will share three quarters of the estate. What remains (*quotité disponible*) can be allocated according to the terms of the will (e.g. left to the surviving spouse or the cats' home).

Example

In the case of a property worth €300,000, owned on a 50/50 basis by a couple with two children, the situation on the first death would look like this:

Survivor	€150,000	(his own share of the property)
Child 1	€50,000	(1/3 deceased's share)
Child 2	€50,000	(1/3 deceased's share)

The remainder of the deceased's share (€50,000) could be willed, if desired, to the surviving spouse who now owns the property jointly with the children. A spouse (but *not* an unmarried partner) has a right to a lifetime use of the property; but any decision on its disposal will have to be made with the children's agreement.

While the French are quite accustomed to such an arrangement it can come as a nasty shock to an unsuspecting non-resident property owner. Non-residents are not exempt from the French Civil Code.

So what is the foreign property buyer to do if he wishes to avoid such an outcome? There are three possible solutions:

TONTINE

The simplest (and nil cost) answer is to have a tontine clause inserted in the title deeds at the time of purchase. The property then passes to the survivor as though the deceased partner never owned it. This avoids the whole issue of the rights of children (including children of previous marriages) or other relatives. However, there are two disadvantages which should be taken into account:

- The tontine clause must be written in to the title deeds by the *notaire* when the property is bought. The deeds cannot be altered later to include it.

- Like a joint tenancy in the UK both parties have to agree in order to sell the property. Neither can force a sale.

COMMUNAUTÉ UNIVERSELLE

The French have two kinds of marriage regime – one in which the parties each hold their own possessions separately (*séparation des biens*) and one in which they jointly own some or all of their possessions (*communauté universelle*). This is of considerable importance to married foreign property buyers.

The Hague Convention (*Convention de la Haye*) of 14 March 1978 (in force in France from 1 September 1992) allows foreign nationals, married in another country, to adopt the French matrimonial regime for the purpose of their assets held in France. In other words, they can adopt the *communauté universelle* regime and hold their French property or properties in a common matrimonial 'fund'. They can also stipulate, under this regime, that on the first death the survivor should inherit everything without exception. This is called *attribution de la communauté au survivant*. Children will have no right to inherit until the survivor dies.

The process is remarkably simple. An appointment with a *notaire* is all that is needed. It is best, if possible, to use the *notaire* who acted for the original purchase. In this way it will not be necessary to establish again your country of origin, the date and place of marriage etc. All that he will need to see is your passport.

A simple three-page document is initialled, signed and witnessed. Article one of this document states that the parties wish to adopt the *communauté universelle* regime, as allowed under the Hague Convention, solely for the properties they own in France.

Article two states that this is in accordance with article 1526 of the French Civil Code, that the change affects both properties currently owned and any future purchases and that it relates only to properties situated in France. It specifically states that the parties do not wish to change their original matrimonial regime in relation to properties held outside France.

Article three, headed *attribution de la communauté au survivant*, states that, on the first death, everything, without exception (*sans aucune exception ni réserve*), passes to the survivor in accordance with articles 1524 and 1525 of the Civil Code. Specifically, the heirs of the deceased have no claim on the property.

Once the document is signed and witnessed it has immediate effect.

Points to note:

1. It is only available to married couples.

2. It can be arranged at any time and does not have to be in place at the time of purchase. It can therefore be organised many years after the purchase.

3. It is not a cheap option. Expect to pay about €800.

4. Once in place, all future property purchases are automatically included. No further adjustments are required.

5. Where there are children from previous marriages this is not the appropriate option. Such children continue to have rights and can apply to the French courts to enforce them. It is therefore only suitable for a married couple who do *not* have children from previous marriages.

6. The agreement of both parties is needed to sell the property.

FRENCH COMPANY

In the UK it is possible to buy property through a limited company. This will usually be a 'special purpose vehicle' or SPV set up solely for the purpose of buying and managing property (buy-to-let lenders will not normally accept any other arrangement for the purpose of a mortgage). In France there is a similar company structure called *Société Civile Immobilière* (SCI). As in the UK the company itself is a separate legal entity and it is the company that owns the property (the company directors own shares in the company).

The SCI is strictly non-trading and its sole purpose is to buy and manage property on a non-commercial basis. Buying property to resell is a commercial activity. Buying property to let furnished (as opposed to unfurnished) is also considered commercial. Holiday letting is therefore not possible. If the SCI strays into either of these activities it will incur French corporation tax. For this reason the company statutes will normally rule these out.

The significance of the SCI for property purchase lies in the fact that it is the company shares, not the property, that are passed on to the shareholders' heirs. Shares, unlike property, are not 'immovable' and thus not covered by French succession law. It is the inheritance law of the country of *residence* that applies. Accordingly the problems associated with French inheritance law are avoided, including the issue of the rights of children from previous marriages. Shares can be left to anyone.

Another advantage of the company structure is that it allows for multiple owners (not necessarily related) and for the inclusion of children as well as their parents.

Points to note:

1. No shareholder can force the sale of the property or dissolution of the company. Conversely, all shareholders have to agree on

any course of action, such as the sale of the property. This could present problems where there are many shareholders in the company.

2. If property is bought for the purpose of holiday letting or furnished letting this is definitely *not* the option to choose (see above).

3. For a married couple, with no children from previous marriages, probably *not* the best option.

4. The cost of setting up an SCI, through a *notaire*, is significant. Allow for €2000–€2500.

5. An SCI is neither cheap nor simple to operate. Accounts need to be kept and audited, annual tax returns made, annual general meetings held and minuted. The services of an accountant will almost certainly be needed.

6. If using an SCI for property purchase care has to be taken to set it up well in advance of any offer or *compromis de vente* (see Chapter 6). It is the company that makes the offer, signs the contracts and buys the property. Accordingly it is vital to consult a *notaire* before embarking on the search for a property.

7. Using an SCI does not avoid inheritance tax even though the shares themselves are not 'immovable'.

8. Professional advice is absolutely essential both for the legal and tax implications of using an SCI.

CONCLUSION

There are quite distinct advantages and drawbacks in all three options – *tontine*, *communauté universelle*, SCI. Care needs to be taken that the route chosen is best suited to your needs.

As a general rule, a married couple with no children from previous marriages should consider *communauté universelle*. If they have children from a previous marriage the *tontine* option may be preferable. An unmarried couple buying jointly should also consider a *tontine*. For multiple buyers (related or not) who intend to let unfurnished the SCI may be the most practical route.

6

The Legal Process

Buying a property in the UK is a slow, uncertain business with no party legally committed until contracts are exchanged, in most cases months after the initial offer has been accepted. At any time during this process either party can pull out without penalty. As a result, gazumping and gazundering are always possible. In France the situation could not be more different. While it can take just as long to complete the purchase, both sides in the French system are legally bound almost from the beginning. Gazumping and gazundering are virtually unknown. The British buyer needs to be fully alert to this from the start.

Having located a suitable property the would-be buyer, as in the UK, will be invited to make an offer. An estate agent will normally ask for this in writing.

THE OFFER (*offre d'achat*)

Great care needs to be taken with the wording of this offer (sometimes called *promesse d'achat*). It will not do simply to write: *I offer to buy property x for y euros.* If an offer like this is accepted in writing the deal is finalised. An effort should be made to retain as much room for manoeuvre as possible.

- Make the offer subject to acceptance within a specific time (e.g. seven days). If the vendor doesn't respond in this time the offer lapses.

▓ If a mortgage is required to make the purchase it is important to mention this now (as well as later in the preliminary contract). The offer should be contingent on acquiring the mortgage.

▓ To buy some more time make the offer subject to the signing of the preliminary contract which is to follow. This, in turn, has a seven-day cooling-off period (see below).

A deposit is not required at this stage and it is illegal to ask for one. If money changes hands the offer is invalid. If the vendor replies with an alternative price the offer is invalidated and cannot be enforced.

PRELIMINARY CONTRACT

The process now moves briskly to the next stage – the preliminary contract, called *promesse de vente* or *compromis de vente* (when buying off-plan the preliminary contract or *contrat de réservation* is quite different and is dealt with separately in Chapter 8). This can happen within days of the offer being accepted. It can be drawn up by a *notaire* but is more commonly provided by the estate agent handling the sale.

Promesse de vente/Compromis de vente

Somewhat confusingly, the French have two preliminary contracts and there is a subtle but significant difference between them. The *promesse de vente* is a promise by the vendor to sell the property to the buyer within a certain specified time (e.g. three months) if the buyer chooses to buy it. The buyer has a seven-day cooling-off period during which he can change his mind and withdraw from the transaction altogether (see below). After this, however, he is committed and required to pay a deposit of 10% to the *notaire*. If he subsequently chooses *not* to proceed (although all specified conditions in the contract are met) he forfeits his deposit. If the vendor, for his part, changes his mind and refuses to sell within the agreed time frame the buyer can sue him for damages but, crucially, cannot force him to sell. For most buyers this is an unsatisfactory outcome. If the vendor is to be compelled to sell the property the *notaire* must insert a clause in the *promesse de vente* specifically requiring him to do so.

The *compromis de vente* is a more straightforward version of the preliminary contract. Once the cooling-off period has passed (and provided other specified conditions in the contract are met) the buyer is obliged to complete. Unlike the *promesse de vente*, however, he will not simply lose his deposit. He can be compelled to buy the property! The vendor is likewise obliged to sell. This is generally considered more satisfactory all round and the *compromis de vente* is the most commonly used preliminary contract. In Paris, however, the *promesse de vente* is still popular with notaries and estate agents.

Cooling-off period

Given the crucial importance of the preliminary contract (referred to as a 'private agreement' or *acte sous seing privé*) in the French conveyancing system it should only be signed after very careful consideration. Mistakes, however, can be made and a purchaser can change his mind. The French system allows for this by providing a seven-day period of reflection, after signing the contract, during which the purchaser can change his mind and legally withdraw. No reason needs to be given. Until recently this opportunity to cancel (*délai de rétractation*) applied only to the purchase of new properties. Since 1 June 2001, however, when the law *Solidarité et Renouvellement Urbain* (SRU) came into force, it applies to all properties.

The contract in detail

There is a set format for preliminary contracts and much of the content is devoted to a statement of the essential elements of the sale, in very precise detail – name and address of the vendor (*vendeur*), name and address of the purchaser (*acquéreur*), full address of the property, full description of the property (bedrooms, bathroom etc.), the exact size or floor area (*superficie*) of the property along with the name, address and qualifications of the person who took the measurements, the lot number if the property is part of a co-ownership or *copropriété* (see Chapter 7), the price to be paid and whether the purchaser will pay the agent's fees.

Names and addresses of the *notaire* and the selling agent must also be included. If the property is an apartment in a co-ownership (*copropriété*) contact details of the management company (*syndic*) for the building will also be provided.

When buying an apartment in a *copropriété* (Chapters 7 and 16) the purchaser knows that charges will be levied for repairs and maintenance to the common areas of the building. What he will not know is whether works have recently been carried out which have yet to be paid for or whether a decision has been made to carry out works in the future. The contract specifies that the vendor will pay for works already carried out. For works proposed, but not yet carried out, the parties can decide who is to pay. The works must be specified and the party named. If this matter is not addressed then the purchaser will have to pay if he is in ownership when the charge for the works is levied.

Other basic details include the vendor's confirmation that he has full title to the property and that there is no mortgage on it (or, if there is, that he will obtain a certificate of redemption from the lender). He will also state if the property is being sold with vacant possession or with a sitting tenant (in the latter case details of the tenancy will be annexed to the contract). He confirms that he is unaware of any town planning restrictions in relation to the property.

Health and safety issues feature prominently in the contract, with sections devoted to asbestos (*amiante*), lead poisoning (*saturnisme*) and termites (*termites*).

In the case of possible asbestos contamination 1 July 1997 is an important date. Buildings constructed after that date present no risk and the vendor need only tick the appropriate box. If it was built prior to that date, however, the vendor is required to produce a full report (*constat*) at the time of signing the preliminary contract. This report will specify whether there is asbestos in the building or not, where exactly it is located (if it is present) and how it is being treated or rendered safe. Any technical reports on the matter must be produced.

With regards to lead in the building the cut-off date is the year 1948. If the building was constructed later than this there is no issue. If it was built before this *and if*, according to the local *préfecture*, it is situated in an area at risk from lead contamination, then a report (dated no less than one year before the contract is signed) must be provided, in compliance with article L.1334-5 of the *Nouveau Code de la Santé Publique*.

As for termites, the vendor can claim to have no knowledge of their existence. Alternatively he can admit that they do indeed exist but that the town hall has been made aware of the situation. Lastly, he has the option to declare that the building is in an area at risk from infestation. In this case a full report will be required, dated within three months of the sale completion date. If such a report is not provided and termites are subsequently found in the building the contract can be declared null and void.

While much of this may seem of minor significance to a potential buyer the section in the preliminary contract devoted to possible opt-out conditions (*conditions suspensives*) should be seen as hugely important and should be treated with very great care. If any of these conditions are not met the buyer can walk away from the contract without penalty.

Opt-out conditions (*conditions suspensives*)

Certain conditions are automatically included and listed in the contract. They are: that there is no planning information to suggest the building is unfit for its intended use, that any mortgage on the property does not exceed the price being paid for it and that the local authority does not exercise its right of pre-emption (*droit de préemption*) and step in to buy the property itself. In the event of any of these conditions being unsatisfied the parties to the contract are no longer bound by it.

In addition to these the purchaser can state his own condition or conditions in the contract (a section is set aside for this, headed *autres conditions suspensives*). If they are not fulfilled he will have the right to withdraw without penalty. These conditions can cover anything at all which the purchaser considers essential, such as a requirement that the vendor fix the leaking roof or that the searches reveal no planning application for a pig farm next door.

By far the most common condition, however, is that the buyer succeed in getting a mortgage for the purchase.

The mortgage condition

It is difficult to overstate this condition. The reason French estate agents love foreign buyers is that they frequently have no need for a French mortgage. The greatest risk of a sale falling through (failure to get a mortgage) is instantly eliminated.

Rules regarding mortgage finance and the preliminary contract are set out in detail in the *Loi Scrivener* which deals with all property-related loans above €21,343.

The Act states that the buyer is not bound by the contract he has signed if he cannot obtain the mortgage he needs. He is entitled to the refund of his deposit. On the other hand, it also stipulates that he must complete the purchase if a lender provides the mortgage specified in the contract. If it can be shown that the purchaser deliberately impeded the mortgage application by, for example, providing false information about his income, he is deemed to be in default and the vendor can exact the penalties stated in the contract. If, through no fault of his own, a period of four months has elapsed without a response from a lender, the purchaser is no longer bound by the contract.

Crucially, if there is no mention of a mortgage in the contract, and the purchaser decides to look for one after all, he may still be protected provided he has not made a handwritten declaration in the contract to the effect that he would *not* be seeking a loan. For this reason there is a section in the contract devoted solely to such a declaration and headed *DECLARATION MANUSCRITE de L'ACQUÉREUR*. Here the purchaser must copy, *in his own handwriting,* a preprinted statement (in French, of course) to the effect that he is making the purchase without recourse to a loan and that he has been informed that should he change his mind and seek a loan after all he will not be able to make this mortgage a condition of the purchase. The French text, which must be copied verbatim, typically reads as follows:

Je soussigné (nom et prénom) déclare effectuer cette acquisition sans recourir à aucun prêt. Je reconnais avoir été informé que si je recours néanmois à un prêt je ne pourrai me prévaloir de la condition suspensive de son obtention prevue au livre 111 chapitre 11 du code de la consommation relatif au crédit immobilier.

If, on the other hand, a French mortgage is needed for the purchase the contract will require very precise details as the vendor will need to know exactly what is proposed and the timescale envisaged. The following mortgage details will be included in the contract:

- The lender who will be approached for the mortgage

- The amount required

- The mortgage product, the interest rate, the term

- The date by which the application will be submitted

- The anticipated date of approval

It is clear that the preliminary contract should not be signed without first making initial enquiries with a lender, either directly or through a broker. Ideally a decision in principle will already be in place before a preliminary contract is presented for signature.

The purchaser will be expected to pursue his mortgage exactly as set out in the contract. If he can be shown to obstruct the process in any way and, as result, fails to get a mortgage, he stands to lose his deposit.

If the mortgage is declined the buyer is entitled to withdraw from the contract and recover his deposit. He will, however, be expected to provide evidence of this in the form of a letter from the lender who rejected the application.

THE DEPOSIT

In the UK the deposit is paid on exchange of contracts, usually months after the initial offer has been made and accepted. In France the deposit (10%) is paid when the preliminary contract is signed. It should always be handed over to the *notaire* (not the estate agent or the vendor) who will open a special client account (*compte client*) for this purpose. It will then form part of the sale price. If the sale is abandoned (because one of the *conditions suspensives* has not been fulfilled) the deposit is returned to the buyer.

THE *NOTAIRE*

With the preliminary contract out of the way and the deposit handed over, the *notaire* takes centre stage. For the buyer accustomed to dealing with the English conveyancing solicitor, the *notaire* is a strange figure in the process. It will come as a surprise to learn that he represents neither the buyer nor the seller! He is a public official, representing the state. His task is to ensure the legality of the transaction. He will also collect any outstanding property taxes and pass these on to the appropriate government department. Before the final contract is signed he

Tips

Although it is not necessary to do so, sign the preliminary contract in the presence of a notaire. Most estate agents will provide the contract and ask you to sign it (having filled it in for you in advance!) but none will explain its implications. As can be seen from the above there is a good deal to consider and the notaire is obliged to ensure that everything you need is included in the contract and that you understand what you are signing.

If a mortgage is required make sure this is stated clearly as a condition of the purchase.

If there are any other important conditions make sure these are listed under 'autres conditions suspensives' (see above).

If the contract is a 'promesse de vente' discuss with the notaire the insertion of a clause extending the vendor's liability (see above).

If the property is an apartment in a co-ownership or copropriété (see Chapter 7) check carefully if works yet to be carried out (already voted on at a general meeting) are listed in the contract. Whoever is in ownership at the time the charge is levied will be expected to pay. The parties can, however, agree a different arrangement. If a new roof is planned either you or the vendor will have to pay for it. Agree this point with the vendor before signing.

Pay the deposit to the notaire only.

will ensure that the parties understand what is happening and that the terms of the preliminary contract are fully met. When the contract is finally sealed with the *notaire*'s stamp it has the full force of law. For additional security all notaries have professional indemnity insurance. There is no equivalent to the *notaire* in the British legal system.

Between the signing of the preliminary contract and the final contract the *notaire* must verify the identity of the parties and satisfy himself that the vendor has a valid title to the property.

To this end the purchaser is required to complete a 'Civil Status Form' providing full name, date and place of birth, occupation, nationality, address, marital status, dates of birth and names of any children. If married, he must state where the marriage took place and provide the same details for his spouse. A copy of his passport must be returned with the form (the original passport will be examined later).

The land registry will be searched to check title to the property. This information will be cross-checked with the preliminary contract and the title deeds. Care will be taken to ensure the vendor is not prevented in any way from selling the property (*absence de restriction à son droit de disposer*).

The *notaire* will then turn his attention to other details in the preliminary contract. Supporting documents for lead, asbestos and termite presence in the building will be examined. Information relating to the *copropriété* (see Chapter 7) if applicable, will be checked. Care will be taken to ensure that the all important opt-out conditions are fully met. He will obtain confirmation that the local authority will not exercise its right to buy the property (*droit de préemption*).

Legal fees (*frais de notaire*)

While the *notaire* is a public official he is not paid by the state. His fees are paid by the purchaser. The level of fees, however, is set by the state and varies with the price of the property. Typically, 6% to 8% overall can be expected. For new-build properties and properties under five years old the fees are lower (3% to 5%). These figures include the *notaire*'s own remuneration and assorted other expenses or disbursements (*débours*) such as land registry costs, fees to surveyor (*géomètre*) for providing measurements, local taxes, cost of registering a mortgage, photocopying, stamps etc. If no mortgage is involved the cost drops by about 1%.

The *notaire*'s remuneration (*honoraires du notaire*) within these figures varies with the price of the property. On the first €6,500 of the price he can charge 4%. Between €6,500 and €17,000 this drops to 1.65%. Between €17,000 and €30,000 the fee is 1.10%. On the amount above €30,000 the charge is 0.825%. This sort of variable remuneration is called *émoluments proportionnels* and will be listed as such in the *notaire*'s completion statement (*état de frais*).

It should be noted that if a French mortgage is required the *notaire*'s fee cannot be added to the sum borrowed. It must be paid by the buyer.

For a website that provides a useful ready reckoner calculation of likely costs in a property purchase, see *Legal Costs Calculation* in Appendix C. For this you will need the following details: the purchase price, the number of the *département* in which the property is situated, whether a mortgage is being used for the purchase and whether the property is more than five years old.

One *notaire* or two?

The *notaire* instructed by the vendor (usually on the recommendation of the selling agent) represents neither party in the transaction and is strictly impartial. There is nothing, however, to prevent the purchaser from instructing his own *notaire* to act on his behalf. Surprisingly, there is no additional cost involved. The two *notaires* share the fee! There is a clear advantage if the second *notaire* is English-speaking. There may also be circumstances in which the purchaser could call on his *notaire* for assistance if an unexpected problem arises. If, for example, there is a last minute delay in transferring funds from the UK (with the risk of missing the deadline for completion) the purchaser's *notaire* might be able to negotiate a brief extension.

For details on how to find an English-speaking *notaire*, see Appendix C.

UK lawyer?

There are specialist lawyers in the UK who advise on the purchase of French property (a Google web search will locate a reasonable selection). While they can't act on their clients' behalf they can explain the legal process involved, request a copy of the final contract in advance and explain it in detail before the buyer sets out to sign it in France. They can also offer advice on other related matters such as income and inheritance tax. Their fees will, however, be an extra cost in the transaction.

FINAL CONTRACT (*acte de vente*)

The final contract is, in effect, the full and definitive version of the preliminary contract. All the documents the *notaire* has obtained since the preliminary contract was signed are included.

There are lengthy reports on the presence or otherwise of termites, lead and asbestos in the building, with detailed entries for hallway, bedrooms, living room, bathroom and kitchen. Also enclosed will be documents relating to town planning and the right of preemption, a map from the land registry office showing the area and location of the property.

If the property is an apartment in a *copropriété* (see Chapter 7) the *notaire* will have obtained a final statement of account from the management company, showing any sums still due to be paid by the vendor. This statement will be included along with reports, if available, of the last two general meetings. Any modifications to the rules of the *copropriété* will be listed, along with details and dates. Also listed will be details of the current insurance cover on the building, any debts or holdings of the management committee, any notices served on the building (e.g. declaring it unsafe or a threat to public health), declarations regarding the presence or otherwise of lead, asbestos and termites in the building.

In the UK it is common for the buyer to sign the contract and post it back to his solicitor. In due course he will receive a letter to the effect that contracts have been exchanged and a date for completion agreed. Eventually he will receive confirmation in the post that the transaction has been completed. He will have met neither the vendor, the vendor's solicitor nor the estate agent. He may not even have clapped eyes on his *own* solicitor! Everything can be conducted impersonally, by post. In France, things are very different.

The signing of the final contract at the *notaire*'s office is quite an event and is taken very seriously. The date is known well in advance and all parties must attend. These are the buyer and seller, the *notaire* or *notaires*, the selling agent and, where required, an interpreter (the contract itself is in French and proceedings will be conducted throughout in French. See below). If the buyer or seller cannot attend he must appoint someone to take his place, giving him power of attorney to do so (see below). *La Poste* has no part to play in the proceedings!

Power of attorney

If it is not possible to attend, someone can be authorised to act on behalf of the absentee (this applies also in the case of the preliminary contract). A standard form is completed and signed, naming the substitute (*mandataire*) and giving him power of attorney (*procuration*) to act. The power is limited and the form will state precisely what he is empowered to do (e.g. signing a preliminary contract or final contract in relation to the purchase of the designated property at the stated price). Additional details of importance (e.g. that the purchase is being made without a mortgage) may also be mentioned.

Interpreter

It is unusual to find a *notaire* who is both fluent in English and willing to translate for the benefit of the buyer. Instead, the services of an interpreter are routinely offered if the purchaser requires one. The interpreter's fee is paid by the purchaser.

Purchase funds

Before the formalities begin the *notaire* checks that the balance of the purchase price has actually arrived – either in the form of mortgage from a French lender or funds transferred from the buyer's UK account to the *notaire's*. If for any reason this is not the case the whole proceedings are called off and the buyer is technically in breach of contract.

The signing

Nothing is left to chance at the signing. The *notaire* goes through each page of the contract separately (it is not bound at this stage), then passes each page round the table for the parties to initial. Given the voluminous contents of a typical contract this can take some time. When everything is complete the estate agent formally hands over the keys and the notaire gives the vendor a cheque for the proceeds of the sale.

At this point the buyer does not receive the deed of sale. The authenticated copy (*copie authentique*) follows six months later (this time in the post), duly signed and stamped by the *notaire*. In the meantime the *notaire* issues a certificate (*attestation*) to confirm completion.

Other formalities

The property has now changed hands and the new owner's responsibilities start immediately.

Insurance on the property must be arranged straight away (see Chapter 10).

The agent will have contact details for the utility companies currently supplying the property. These should be advised immediately of the change of ownership.

Lastly, there is the matter of the occupancy tax or *taxe d'habitation* (see Chapter 24). This is paid in January for the whole year. As the vendor will already have paid this tax for the year he will look to the purchaser to reimburse him the amount overpaid. The vendor will normally have calculated the amount in advance and will settle this privately with the buyer.

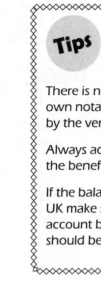

There is no disadvantage and no extra cost in instructing your own notaire to act on your behalf, alongside the notaire chosen by the vendor. Always take this option.

Always accept the offer of an interpreter. The cost is modest and the benefits considerable.

If the balance of the purchase price has to be transferred from the UK make sure this is done in plenty of time to reach the notaire's account before the signing. A minimum of five working days should be allowed.

7

Buying an Apartment

While buying a freehold property in the UK is a relatively straightforward business, buying a leasehold flat is certainly not. There are many issues to be considered:

How many years are left on the lease? Can the lease be extended? Is the apartment a conversion or part of a purpose-built block? Is 'share-of-freehold' available? If a conversion, what are the arrangements for the upkeep of the building? Is there a sinking fund? If a purpose-built block is there a management company and where are they located? What are the management charges? What is the ground rent? Are the other leaseholders trying to buy out the freehold?

Things are a great deal simpler than this in France.

THE *COPROPRIETE*

A peculiarity of the French property market is the elaborate and rigidly regulated system of co-ownership or *copropriété* (established by law on 10 July 1965) which applies to all apartment buildings in France. The British system of leasehold apartments, with a separate freehold of the building, owned by someone else, is unknown. Instead, each co-owner (*copropriétaire*) has his own share (*quote-part*) of the common parts of the building as well as exclusive right to his apartment without limit of time.

The essential features of the *copropriété* are as follows:

Management committee

The management committee (*le syndic*) is appointed by the members and draws an expenses allowance approved each year at the annual general meeting. A *syndic* cannot stay in office for more than three years and is usually appointed for one year, renewable. Decisions taken at general meetings are carried out by the *syndic*.

General meetings

A general meeting must be held at least once a year. Each *copropriétaire* has to be notified by registered post 21 days in advance of the meeting. If he can't attend he can use a form provided to appoint a representative with power of attorney (*mandataire*) to take his place. This can be anyone of his choice, apart from a spouse or employee. Everyone signs in and an attendance sheet (*feuille de présence*) is kept and added to the minutes (*procès-verbal*) of the meeting. A full agenda is provided.

The votes allocated to each *copropriétaire* are in proportion to his share or *quote-part* (see below). Should a single *copropriétaire* have a share which is more than half the total his voting strength is reduced to match that of all the others together. Most matters relating to the management of the building are the subject of a simple majority vote of those present at the meeting. In some cases, however, an absolute majority of all members, whether present or not, will be required. This would be necessary, for example, for the election or dismissal of the *syndic* or to decide on the introduction of water meters for all. A unanimous vote of all would be required for any change to the shares of the *copropriétaires*.

Share calculation

For this purpose the *copropriété* is divided into thousandths (*millièmes*) and each owner is allocated a share, expressed as a percentage (*tantième*) of the whole. The number of thousandths allocated to a co-owner will depend on the size (and hence the value) of his apartment compared to the others in the building. This has a direct bearing on the charges levied for the upkeep of the common areas. The owner of a small studio will pay a great deal less than the owner of a spacious three bedroom apartment. It also affects the voting strength of the *copropriétaires* at general meetings (see above).

Rules and regulations

Every *copropriété* has a set of rules (*règlement de copropriété*) and every new owner is provided with a copy by the *notaire* at the completion of the purchase. If the owner lets the apartment he is expected to supply his tenant with a copy.

The rule book sets out in considerable detail the rights and duties of the *copropriétaires*. It will cover a wide range of matters, including activities which are strictly forbidden (such as hanging one's washing out the window or playing loud music at night), the responsibility of owners to maintain properly the front door to their apartment (and any front door mat) and details of annual general meetings (with the rights of the *copropriétaires* to attend and vote).

Particular attention is paid to the sort of alterations to the apartment (or *lot* as it is referred to) which are permissible and those which require the authorisation of the *syndic* at a meeting of the general assembly. As a general rule anything that impacts on the common areas of the building or affects the exterior of the building would fall into this category. The installation of air conditioning is a case in point.

The rules may expressly forbid the use of the apartment for running a business or it may allow this and set out the conditions under which it can take place.

Crucially, the rule book contains a list of all *lots* by number in the building, the location of each and the share (*quote-part*) that each has for the purpose of maintenance and repair costs of the common areas.

Charges

The upkeep of the building and associated administrative costs need to be paid for and all *copropriétaires* must contribute according to their share or *quote-part*. The level of charges can vary significantly from one apartment building to another and will depend on the facilities and services provided. The charges levied in a modern apartment block with lift, swimming pool and tennis courts will be a great deal higher than those in an unmodernised building in, say, the Old Town of Nice. Charges are normally levied quarterly.

Items covered are typically cleaning, electricity bills for the common areas, roof repairs, cost of holding general meetings, expenses paid to members of the *syndic* (see above) etc. Other costs could cover services which all can benefit from, such as a lift, communal heating, rubbish chutes, swimming pool etc. It is the availability of these services that matters, not whether they are actually used (the exception being ground floor residents who would not be charged for the lift).

Tips

When viewing an apartment pay as much attention to the building as to the apartment itself. First impressions on the upkeep of the building will reveal a great deal. If there is little evidence of cleaning, decoration or general maintenance then you may well wonder what will happen to the management charges you will have to pay. You can redecorate and refurbish the apartment but you rely on the syndic to maintain the building. The state of the common areas will also tell you a good deal about your future neighbours. Graffiti on the walls, discarded cigarette butts or the smell of urine in the stairwell will tell you all you need to know. The most assiduous of syndics will achieve little under such circumstances.

The level of charges is clearly a matter of some importance and the estate agent should be pressed for precise details in this regard. A description of the charges as 'faibles' or low should not be accepted. Given the fees the agent will earn on the sale it is perfectly reasonable to expect him to make a few enquiries on your behalf. At the very least the charges for the last few years should be made available.

If future works to the building are planned (at a future cost to yourself) you will normally hear about these only at the very last minute – just before you sign the final contract. The syndic may not feel obliged to provide these details to your agent (they are legally obliged to notify the notaire) but it is worthwhile asking for them.

As the rules relating to these charges are enshrined in law any *copropriétaire* can object if he considers them to be unfair and, if he fails to get satisfaction, take the matter to court. He can also demand to see the record of maintenance and repairs *carnet d'entretien* which all *copropriétés* are obliged to keep and make available on demand to apartment owners.

Should a *copropriétaire* fail to pay his charges by the due date the *syndic* has authority to take immediate action. A registered letter is dispatched, formally demanding payment. If, after 30 days, payment has not been made the *syndic* can take legal action, through a specially accelerated procedure, to obtain payment. If judgement is obtained in their favour and the defendant still fails to pay, the bailiffs can be sent in to seize his goods and sell them to recover the debt and all associated legal costs. If the defendant wins, however, the costs must be borne by the *syndic* and shared among the other copropriétaires.

When an apartment changes hands the *syndic* informs the *notaire* of any payments still owed by the vendor. For the benefit of the purchaser it will indicate if a decision has been taken to carry out any works in the future. The cost of these will normally fall to the owner of the apartment at the time the charge is levied.

8

Buying Off-Plan

Developers in France, like developers everywhere, are anxious to shift stock. Selling off-plan or *vente en l'état futur d'achèvement* (VEFA) is shifting stock before you have it! In this case the developer (*promoteur immobilier*) can solicit prospective buyers although he may, at this point, have neither finance nor planning permission in place and may, indeed, be still negotiating the purchase of the land! If enough buyers can be signed up he will hope to put everything in place and proceed with the development.

Everything therefore depends heavily on advertising and marketing, which is why it is difficult to avoid the advertising blandishments of property developers' agents on property websites and in the property pages of newspapers. Investor clubs too in the UK, hammered by the downturn in the domestic market brought about by the recession, are increasingly turning their attention to foreign off-plan schemes. Should we be tempted?

Why consider off-plan at all? If we are honest, it is probably because we have fallen for the marketing hype about the inevitable increases in value we can expect before the development is even complete. This, we are to believe, is partly due to the substantial discount we are offered on the price and the inevitable rise in unit value as each property in the development is completed. What can possibly go wrong? It took two collapses in the UK property market (early 90s and 2008) to show how dangerously flawed this reasoning can be. In any property downturn off-plan developments are hit hardest of all. Investors whose properties haven't yet been finished are tempted to cut their losses and pull out, while those who have completed on the sale are wishing they hadn't. The whole development can be blighted for years to come. Buying off-plan for investment in the volatile market of the UK has never made much sense.

But could it make sense in France? France has certainly one of the most stable and tightly regulated property markets in Europe and offers a great deal of protection to the off-plan purchaser (see below). The impact of the credit crunch did not cause the same level of devastation and spiralling price collapse experienced in Britain and elsewhere (thanks to the very strict mortgage regime, far fewer buyers were forced to sell, see Chapter 3). The market did, nevertheless, suffer a sharp correction and prices take time to recover. An off-plan purchase in France, as elsewhere, should be strictly for the long term.

As with a standard purchase (see Chapter 6) there are two legal stages in the purchase of an off-plan property – the initial contract, this time called the *contrat de réservation* and the final contract, here referred to as *vente en l'état futur d'achèvement* or VEFA.

Beyond this, however, the process of buying an off-plan property is totally different. There are rules regarding the initial deposit and a strictly regulated system of staged payments throughout the construction. The developer is required to provide a variety of guarantees. Legal fees and tax treatment are different. Finally, there are legal safeguards for the buyer if the finished building does not meet the standards and specifications set out in the contract.

Preliminary Contract

The buyer's commitment to proceed with the purchase is crucial for the developer and he will require a preliminary contract (*contrat de réservation*) to be signed at the outset. A few points are worth noting about this contract:

- It commits the buyer to buy.

- It does not commit the developer to sell!

The developer's position is not quite as unreasonable as it appears. He may not, at this point, have the financial backing he requires. He may not yet have planning permission. You may be the only one, so far, who has expressed any interest in his development! If he can't get sufficient interest, cannot get financial backing or fails to get planning permission then he will have nothing to sell. The initial contract, however, should set out clearly the circumstances in which the developer can pull out of the deal.

For the buyer, at this early stage, there are two standard opt-out clauses, as there are with a normal purchase (see Chapter 6) – cancellation within the seven-day cooling-off period and failure to get a mortgage. In addition to the mortgage condition any number of other *clauses suspensives* can be added, with the agreement of the developer, to cover other matters of importance to the buyer.

While this contract (which has be in writing) is 'preliminary' it must specify the following:

1. Details and specifications of the property to be built. This should include approximate surface area (a legal requirement

under Articles R 261-25 and R 261-26 CHC), number of rooms, type of construction etc. A plan should be provided.

2. Staged payments. The buyer is required to make payments from time to time during the development. The initial contract should say what these payments are and when they are due (see below).

3. What guarantees the developer is providing (see below).

4. The price.

5. The date legal title will pass to the purchaser.

Very precise details may not be provided at this stage and the developer will try to leave himself as much room for manoeuvre as possible. However the purchaser can reasonably expect that the final contract (VEFA) will not differ fundamentally from the initial contract.

THE DEPOSIT

Along with the preliminary contract the developer will require a deposit – *dépôt de garantie*. Like so much else in the process this is strictly regulated:

■   No deposit at all can be asked for or paid until the initial contract is signed.

■   No deposit at all is due if the planned completion date is more than two years away.

■   If the completion date is between one and two years the deposit is 2%.

■ If the completion date is within a year the deposit is 5%. The maximum deposit is therefore lower than the 10% required for a normal purchase (see Chapter 6).

A particular bonus for the purchaser is the knowledge that the developer can have no access to the deposits he collects. These must be kept in a separate account, usually set up by a *notaire* for this purpose. If the completion date (when the VEFA contract is due to be signed) is missed the purchaser can walk away from the deal and demand the return of his deposit.

STAGED PAYMENTS

In the UK off-plan purchasers generally pay a deposit (typically 10%) at the outset and nothing else until completion. In France, however, a system of staged payments applies. This is how it works:

1. Preliminary contract – up to 5% (see above)

2. When foundations are down – 35% of the price

3. When the building is weatherproof – 70% of the price

4. When construction is completed – 95% of price

5. When the keys are handed over – 100% of the price

DEVELOPERS' GUARANTEES

Since the purchaser is required to part with his cash throughout the construction it is reasonable that he should have some assurances. At the very least he will want to know that he will have his money back if the project goes pear-shaped. Ideally he will want a guarantee that the building will be completed, come what may. Builders' guarantees, required by law (*Code de la Construction et d'Habitation*) take two forms:

External guarantee (*garantie extrinsèque*)

This is provided by the bank funding the development. It will either indicate simply that a line of credit has been opened with the developer or – of far greater value – guarantee that the bank will pay to have the development completed if the builder fails to do so.

Personal guarantee (*garantie intrinsèque*)

This is the builder's own guarantee and there are strictly defined circumstances when it can be used, i.e.: (a) the foundations of the building are down and the builder can show he has available to him, from other sources, 75% of the property's sale price; or (b) the building has reached the stage where it is weatherproof and, at the same time, has no outstanding mortgage on it.

The *garantie extrinsèque*, with a guarantee of completion provided by a third party, is clearly the best possible guarantee for the buyer.

THE FINAL CONTRACT

Known as VEFA (*vente en l'état futur d'achèvement*), this is the final, definitive contract (*VEFA définitif*). It must be sent to the purchaser at least a month before the sale (by recorded delivery) so that there is ample time to compare it with the preliminary contract.

It will contain a full account (*notice descriptif*) of all aspects of the planned construction (in addition to the plans provided separately). This will cover technical details of the construction and lists of materials to be used in the foundations, the roof, the walls etc. It is likely, however, that the developer will also add a clause allowing him scope to use equivalent or similar materials to those specified (*clause par équivalent*).

Also specified in the VEFA will be the timescale for completion and delivery, the price, the guarantees provided and the rules of the *copropriété* (*règlement de copropriété*) if the property is to be part of a co-ownership.

Of particular importance are the guarantees. The following should be noted:

Money-back guarantee (*garantie de remboursement*)

This covers the possibility that the development, for whatever reason, never takes place. A bank or insurance company provides the guarantee. The cover is, however, limited to a refund of money paid by the purchaser. It will not ensure the completion of the development.

Guarantee of completion (*garantie d'achèvement*)

The *notaire* will ensure that this guarantee is in place because it is a legal requirement. It ensures that, once building has begun, it will be completed if the builder, for whatever reason, fails to complete it.

Article R 261-23 of the *Code de la Construction et de l'Habitation* allows the developer to begin with the *garantie de remboursement* and switch to the *garantie d'achèvement* at a later stage.

One-year guarantee (*garantie de parfait-achèvement*)

Article 1792-6 of the *Code civil* establishes a legal obligation on the part of the developer to cover all faults for one year after completion. On receipt of a recorded letter from the purchaser, advising him of the fault or faults, he must take steps to put matters right. If he fails to do so he can be taken to the civil court (*tribunal d'instance*). Action needs to be taken within one year of delivery.

Also provided for one year is a guarantee that the building has adequate soundproofing (*isolation phonique*) and conforms to current legal requirements in this regard (article 111-11 chapter 3 of the *Code de la Construction et de l'Habitation*). This applies, however, to the first occupant only. In extreme cases a fault in this area could also be covered by a ten-year guarantee (see below).

Two-year guarantee (*garantie des éléments d'équipements*)

This is a requirement of article 1792-3 of the *Code civil* and provides cover for two years for such non-structural items as windows, doors or carpets. The developer must repair or replace them if necessary (though natural disasters or careless use by the purchaser will free him from this obligation). If the developer doesn't comply, legal action can be taken, within two years of delivery, in the *tribunal d'instance*.

Ten-year guarantee (*garantie décennale*)

This covers structural defects only (and structural related defects such as floors, ceilings and walls). It is a requirement under article 1792 of the *Code civil*. The principle here is that such defects would render the building unfit for purpose (*impropre à sa destination*). The soundproofing (*isolation phonique*) can sometimes be regarded as so inadequate that it renders the building unfit (*impropre à sa destination*). In this case it too would be covered by the ten-year guarantee, instead of by the one-year *garantie de parfait-achèvement* (see above).

In practice the developer takes out an insurance policy (*assurance dommages-ouvrages*) to provide this cover. The purchaser, however, meets the cost of the policy. The developer must have this in place before work starts. A claim is made to the insurance company itself instead of pursuing the builder through the courts. The company has 60 days from receipt of the claim to assess the damage and 30 days after that to make a written offer of payment. The insurance company can be challenged in court if it fails to act within this time frame or rejects a claim without calling for expert opinion. The insurance also extends to a subsequent purchaser of the property on the principle of *l'assurance de chose suit la chose* (the insurance follows the thing insured).

Rights and obligations under VEFA contract

Everything specified in the contract must be carried out and must comply, when completed, with the details in the contract. Where problems arise a distinction needs to be made between faults which are fundamental, such as supplying single glazed windows where double glazing was specified (*défaut de conformité*) and problems relating to the workmanship itself, such as installing windows which don't open or shut (*vice de construction*). In the case of *défaut de conformité* the purchaser need not rely on the guarantees provided. Under French common law (*droit commun*) he has 30 years in which to seek redress. Where the problem is very serious he could refuse to accept delivery altogether until it is put right. At the same time he can withhold the final payment (5%) and place it on deposit with the *notaire* until the developer deals with the problem. If the fault is a *vice de construction* this is covered by the ten-year guarantee.

Notaire's Fees

Legal fees associated with buying off-plan (or buying any property less than five years old) are lower than for an ordinary purchase (see Chapter 6). The *notaire*'s fees will typically be 3% instead of 7%.

Tax and Off-Plan Purchase

There is no local tax (*taxe foncière*) for two years after completion (see Chapter 24). However, unlike the purchase of a property already built (and over five years old), VAT (*TVA*) is charged at 19.6%. This is normally included in the price quoted and is frequently not mentioned at all in marketing literature.

Tips

Off-plan developments, by their very nature, are big. Will there be sufficient demand in the rental market (whether long-term or holiday let) for so many properties coming on-stream at about the same time? It is important to ignore the marketing hype altogether and conduct your own research in the area, paying particular attention to what is already known about the best rental locations (see Chapters 1 and 2).

9

Buying Leaseback

For the off-plan purchaser who is looking for a belt and braces investment, leaseback would seem, at first sight, to be the perfect solution. As the term suggests, the property, when purchased, is 'leased back' to the developer or, more usually, to a property management company. The company undertakes to find tenants for the property (usually on a holiday letting basis) and provides the owner with a guaranteed rent, whether the property is let or not.

As if that weren't enough, the VAT (*TVA*) paid on the purchase (19.6%) is refunded to the investor (this is in addition to the two years' exemption from local property tax applicable to any off-plan purchase). This concession on *TVA*, however, is not quite what it seems at first sight as the rental income on these properties will be subject to a 5.5% *TVA* charge, thus enabling the treasury to recover its *TVA* over a 20-year period. Nevertheless it certainly encourages developers to apply for authorisation to build *résidences de tourisme*, or government approved holiday complexes, in areas earmarked for development. They are usually located near ski slopes, golf courses or in popular coastal areas. The holiday companies that run such complexes belong to the *Syndicat National des Résidences de Tourisme* (SNRT), a body that oversees their activities and encourages best practice (see Appendix C).

All this is made possible by the French government's active role in promoting the tourist industry.

The essential features of leaseback purchase are as follows:

1. The property is leased to the management company for a minimum period of nine years. While nine years is the norm, a term of 11 years is not uncommon. At the end of the lease the company has an option to renew for a further 11 years (where the first lease was for nine years) or for a further nine years (where the first lease was for 11). The total lease term could therefore be 20 years. At the end of the term the property must be returned in good condition.

2. The company is responsible for furnishing the property and meeting all day-to-day management and maintenance costs.

3. A guaranteed rent of between 3% and 6% of the purchase price (sometimes inclusive of *TVA*) is paid to the owner, whether the property is rented or not. The rent is indexed to inflation and is paid net of management costs.

4. The owner has an agreed number of weeks per year during which he can use the property himself. The number of weeks is agreed at the outset, with a maximum period set at six months. The level of guaranteed rent, however, is linked to the time chosen for personal use, with a lower level paid for longer periods chosen. There is no cost for personal use during the allocated times but if additional periods are required these would normally have to be paid for, though usually at a discounted rate.

5. VAT (*TVA*) paid on the off-plan purchase is refunded. However, this refund is conditional on the property being kept for 20 years. If it is sold before the 20 years are up, a proportion of the *TVA* (a twentieth for each year remaining) will have to be repaid. This will also be the case if the owner decides to live in the property or let it privately.

The attractions of the leaseback arrangement are obvious – a fully furnished and equipped property, guaranteed rent, a juicy tax refund and nothing at all to do!

For the UK investor there is the additional advantage that a French leaseback purchase can be placed in a UK Self Invested Personal Pension (SIPP), making both rental income and capital gain tax free (professional advice is essential here).

There are, however, some drawbacks which should be considered:

- A nine-year lease (or 20 if the holiday company exercises its option to renew) may be too long for many people.

- At the end of the leaseback period it is likely that many properties will be coming on the market (either to sell or to let) at about the same time. This may adversely affect the rental or sale price that might be achieved.

- The property can be sold before the lease runs out but it must be sold with the existing lease in place. This will reduce considerably the number of potential buyers and will adversely affect the resale price. As mentioned above, a proportion of the VAT (*TVA*) originally refunded will also have to be repaid.

- In many cases the guaranteed rent may not cover the mortgage payments, especially where there is a high loan-to-value and the mortgage is on a capital and interest basis. See Chapter 3.

While the rent is guaranteed the management company providing this rent is not! It can go out of business. No company, no rent. This is most likely to happen if the location is poorly chosen and does not have the rental demand to make the project profitable in the long term. For this reason the track record of the company itself should be thoroughly checked and the chosen location carefully researched.

10

Property Insurance

Once the purchase is made there is a legal requirement in France to insure the property. This will be arranged when the final contract is signed. While the policy itself will not yet be available, a certificate of insurance (*attestation d'assurance*) will be faxed to the *notaire*. The certificate will indicate the areas of cover provided. At a minimum these will include damage caused by fire, explosion and flood (*incendie, explosions, dégâts des eaux*) and third party liability (*recours des voisins et des tiers*).

For the property investor, however, this is not as simple as it sounds. If the insurer is not aware that the property is to be let there may, in reality, be no cover at all in place! The reason is simply that the insurance risks for a landlord are not the same as for the owner-occupier. A tenant could be injured or die on the premises. He could be responsible for accidental damage to the building or the contents (the landlord's or his own). The situation is further complicated by the legal obligation on some tenants to take out their own insurance and the absence of any such requirement on others (see below). In short, a distinction needs to be drawn between the cover suitable for the owner-occupier, the landlord of unfurnished accommodation and the landlord of a furnished or holiday let property.

THE OWNER-OCCUPIER

As in the UK, the principal risks covered by the standard homeowner property insurance in France (*multirisque habitation*) are buildings, contents and public liability.

In the event of the property being totally destroyed or damaged, buildings insurance covers the cost of rebuilding or repairing it. If a ceiling falls in or the whole building collapses the insurance covers the cost of putting matters right. The only requirement is that the level chosen must be for the full cost of rebuilding the whole property (e.g. €80,000). This should not be confused with the purchase price which may be a great deal higher. If the building is underinsured only a portion of the claim (e.g. 50%) may be met. If the property is mortgaged the lender will normally decide the level of cover required. If there is no mortgage the services of a local surveyor may be required to decide the rebuild cost. It should be noted that in the case of an apartment the building in which it is situated will normally be insured by the management committee. In the event of the whole building being destroyed, therefore, all the apartments would be rebuilt under the block insurance. However, this policy may not cover structural damage to an individual apartment. The rules of the *copropriété* should be scrutinised carefully to establish the level of cover provided.

In addition to buildings cover, public liability insurance (*garantie responsibilité civile*) is included in the policy. This covers the owner in the event of a claim by third parties for loss or injury incurred in the property. The level of cover will run to several million euros. In the case of an apartment the block insurance may provide this cover for the common areas of the building, but not usually for individual apartments. The rules of the *copropriété* will need to be checked.

Contents cover, as an option, is routinely offered. This is normally on a 'new for old' basis (*valeur à neuf*), meaning that if contents or *mobilier* (such as furniture or household appliances) are accidentally damaged, new replacements can be bought. Clothes and linen are sometimes excluded from the 'new for old' formula.

UNFURNISHED LETTING

The same multi-risk policy can be used when the property is let unfurnished, but if the policy has already been taken out *the insurer must be notified in writing* (registered post), without delay, that the property is to be let in this way. Since the tenant must have his own cover for damage caused by fire, flood and explosion (see Chapter 16) the owner's insurer does not bear the full risk. The insurer should be asked to confirm, however, that the owner's public liability cover applies vis-à-vis the tenant.

FURNISHED AND HOLIDAY LET

For the holiday let landlord or landlord of long-term *furnished* property the situation is more complicated. While long-term tenants of unfurnished properties must have their own insurance (see above) there is no similar legal obligation on those who rent furnished properties (see Chapter 17) or on holiday let tenants. Most will have no cover of their own. The insurer needs to be aware of this and the policy itself must be adjusted. If it has already been put in place it is necessary to *notify the insurer in writing* (registered post) that the property is to be let furnished (long-term or holiday let) and that specific endorsements (*clauses personnalisées*) will be required to the policy. These are:

- A statement that the policy holder is covered for public liability (*responsibilité civile*) in respect of death or injury suffered by his tenants. Cover of €4–5m should be provided.

- A clause known as *abandon de recours* to be inserted. This means that the company will not pursue the tenant (i.e. his insurer) in the event of a claim, but will meet the claim itself.

SPECIALIST HOLIDAY LET COVER

There are additional risks to which a holiday let business is exposed and which are not routinely provided for in a French home insurance policy. These are:

Loss of rent

If an accident makes the property uninhabitable during the letting season, weeks or even months of rent will be lost. If bookings have been made and paid for, the rent will have to be refunded. Loss-of-rent cover will provide compensation in these circumstances.

Emergency accommodation

The nightmare scenario for the property owner is a phone call from the agent or cleaner to say that a leak has brought the ceiling down and the holidaymakers have just arrived to collect the keys! The holiday cannot be undone. Emergency accommodation will have to be found and paid for. Insurance can cover the cost.

Emergency travel

In these circumstances an urgent visit by the owner to the disaster scene is clearly called for. Travel and accommodation costs could be significant. These costs can also be insured.

SPECIALIST HOLIDAY LET INSURERS

Comprehensive cover of this kind is not available through French insurance companies but is provided by some UK companies specialising in this area (see Appendix C). Apart from the additional cover provided there are clear advantages for the non-French speaker in dealing with an English company (the policy documents are in English and the process of making a claim will be a great deal easier).

Small print

As with any insurance, however, care needs to be taken with the small print. Holiday let properties can be empty for long periods. Does the insurance company require that the water be cut off in the winter months before it will entertain a claim for water damage? Is there a requirement that the property be inspected on a regular basis or that a minimum temperature be maintained in the winter months? What is the maximum cover provided for lost rent, emergency accommodation and emergency travel? Is there cover for swimming pool accidents? What is the excess (*franchise*) on a claim? Is there a higher excess for certain kinds of claim (e.g. water damage in the off-season)?

Policy cancellation

If the decision is made to replace a policy altogether it should be noted that the cancellation (*résiliation*) of a French policy can only occur if notice is given in writing (registered post) two months before the anniversary date (exceptions are made for moving home or for marital or professional reasons). Otherwise the policy renews automatically. It is unwise to ignore this requirement and simply fail to pay the premium. While the policy will then be cancelled, a declaration to the effect that it was cancelled due to non-payment of the premium must be made in all subsequent home insurance applications, making it difficult or expensive to get cover. Needless to say, the new policy should be in place before the old one is cancelled.

11

French Bank Account

While a bank account in France is not essential for the property purchase itself, it will be near impossible to do without one afterwards. Utility bills, *copropriété* charges etc. have to be paid. A French mortgage lender will expect a direct debit from a French account. The local plumber will take a cheque. There is really no alternative to a French bank account.

OPENING AN ACCOUNT

Opening a current account (*compte à vue* or *compte de dépôt*) in a bank branch will normally involve a brief interview with a relationship manager (*conseiller clientèle*) and the deposit of a small sum in cash. He will require proof of identity in the form of a passport (a residency permit or *carte de séjour* for a non-EU citizen) along with proof of home address, such as a recent utility bill. A signature specimen will be required. If a French property has been bought or rented, proof of the purchase or rental agreement will be required. Banks offer resident and non-resident accounts. The principal difference is that the non-resident account (*compte non-résident*) does not benefit from an overdraft facility.

It is possible to open an account by post so long as the required documentation can be provided. The bank will normally require a copy of the applicant's passport, certified by his own bank, original utility bills or certified copies to prove his current address, a reference from his bank along with two or three months' statements and a cheque or transfer for the opening deposit. Other requirements could include proof of property purchase in France or proof of income.

A formal account agreement (*convention de compte*) will be signed by the manager and account holder. This document sets out the conditions applicable to the account (including charges) along with the rights and duties of both parties. Any modification by the bank to this contract can only be made after two months' notice. Cheque books (*chéquiers*) will be issued in due course, along with a debit card (*carte bleue*). Bank statements (*relevés de compte*) are normally issued monthly.

FEATURES OF THE FRENCH ACCOUNT

The first indication that things are a little different in France comes when the manager hands you a short script (in French) and asks you to copy it out, word for word, on a blank piece of paper, then sign and date it. You have just confirmed, in your own handwriting, that your account will never be overdrawn!

Stay in the black!

There must always be sufficient funds in the account to meet all commitments. In the absence of an agreed overdraft (*découvert*) it is a very serious matter to be overdrawn on a French account. In the case of a bounced cheque the Bank of France (no less!) will be notified of the transgression. If the matter is not rectified within 30 days, cheque books have to be returned and an *interdiction bancaire* (cheque ban) is slapped on the account holder. He will be banned from using cheques for five years. It will not even be possible to sign a cheque as an authorised signatory (e.g. with power of attorney). Failure to comply with the *interdiction* will result in prosecution and a fine. If the account is joint both account holders are affected.

Other inevitable consequences are the cancelling of debit and credit cards, the withdrawal of overdraft facilities and the knock-on effect on the account holder's credit rating – the banking equivalent of being sent to the Bastille! He can continue to have a bank account, but at a very basic level. At best he will have use of a *carte à autorisation systématique*. This is like a debit card but at each transaction the account is automatically checked to ensure sufficient funds are available.

RIB

When an account is opened a statement of the full banking details or *relevé d'identité bancaire* (RIB) is sent to the account holder. Initially this is in the form of a separate slip of paper but will subsequently be attached to bank statements (*relevés de compte*) and cheque books (*chéquiers*).

The RIB contains the name of the account holder, name and location of the bank, sort code (*code banque*), branch code (*code guichet*), account number (*numéro de compte*), bank account code (*clé RIB*), International Bank Account Number (IBAN) and Bank Identifier Code (BIC). In other words, it contains every piece of information relating to the account that might ever be needed. There is nothing equivalent in the UK.

The most common use for the RIB is when paying regular bills without the need for a cheque. A utility company, for example, could attach a TIP (*titre interbancaire de payment*) to its bill. This can be detached, signed and returned. This gives the company permission to take payment directly from the client's account. To set up a TIP arrangement, however, the company first needs sight of an RIB. From that point onwards the TIP will contain all the necessary details and will only need to be signed and dated. The same applies when setting up a direct debit (*prélèvement automatique*) or when making arrangements to receive funds through a bank transfer (*virement*).

Debit card

Like UK banks, French banks provide the account holder with a debit card (*carte bleue*). Based on the chip-and-pin principle the card (usually VISA) can be used to make purchases in shops and withdraw cash from ATMs. Stricter limits are usually imposed, however, than apply in the UK. When it comes to cash withdrawals from an ATM (*distributeur*), there can be a weekly limit (not daily) of as little as €500. In a 30-day period total payments and withdrawals can be capped at €2,500, regardless of the balance of the account to be debited. More generous limits than these have to be negotiated with the bank. In the case of a joint account both account holders receive their own card but, surprisingly, share the same pin number.

Cheques

In France a cheque (*chèque*) is as good as cash. Once written and handed over it can't be stopped (unless it has been lost or stolen). There must always be funds in the account to cover it (see above). The only precaution the recipient may be expected to take is to ask for proof of ID. A cheque remains valid for a year and eight days after it is written.

When writing a French cheque there are some important differences to be noted:

- The first line of the cheque is not for the name of the payee. It is for the amount to be paid. It is headed *payez contre ce chèque*. The amount is then written in words (French words, of course!).

- The section for the payee is below this and begins *à* (to) . . .

- A peculiarity of the French system is the next line which also begins *à* . . . This does not mean 'to' but 'at'. The bank wants to know *where* you are writing the cheque! If you are in London, therefore, you would write *Londres*. If this is left blank the bank will return the cheque.

- The line for the date is marked *le* . . .

- There is no area indicated for a signature but one is required nevertheless. This should be under the date.

- As might be expected, there is a clearly defined box for the amount in figures. Note, however, that the French use a comma (*virgule*), not a decimal point or a dash, to separate the cents from the euros, e.g. €200,25.

Internet banking

For the non-resident internet banking is a great convenience. Instead of having to wait for statements to arrive or endure the ordeal of a telephone call in broken French everything is available at the click of a mouse. Once it is set up all that is needed is a client number (*numéro client*) and a secret code (*code secret*) to access the account.

Bank charges and interest

There is normally no charge for having a basic current account. The bank, however, may charge for specific services such as providing overdrafts or receiving payments from abroad. Apart from appearing on monthly statements these charges must be collated separately on an annual basis (*récapitulatif annuel des frais bancaires*). Paying interest on a current account balance was forbidden altogether until the European Court of Justice ruled this illegal in October 2004. Banks are now free to pay interest, but you might struggle to find one that does!

Joint accounts

An account can be held jointly by two or more accountholders. There are, however, two kinds of joint account and the distinction is important. In the case, for example, of a typical husband and wife account there is a choice of *Monsieur **OU** Madame* or *Monsieur **ET** Madame*. In the first case either account holder can sign documents or cheques. In the second both must sign. The chosen format is printed on each cheque.

All account holders are jointly and severally liable in the eyes of the bank. If the account is in the red, therefore, both *monsieur* and *madame* are liable, even if only one has overspent. Either account holder can close the account (even without the consent of the other) by sending a written request, registered post, to the bank.

WHICH BANK?

When choosing a bank there will be a number of factors to consider, including proximity of a branch to the property, the availability of English-speaking staff and the level of bank charges. If the plan is to buy several properties, choosing a bank with a large number of branches may make sense. While Barclays may be well represented in the Côte d'Azur, there may be no branch nearby in Brittany. The banks with the most branches are BNP Paribas and Crédit Mutuel. Their websites have an English version and in the most popular tourist areas English-speaking staff are frequently available. Crédit Agricole has a dedicated internet and phone banking facility for English-speaking customers – Britline. See Appendix C for a list of French banks.

Part Three

A HOLIDAY LETTING BUSINESS

12

Limiting Risk

For the holiday homeowner who only occasionally lets out his property and is happy to shoulder all costs associated with the purchase, there are few risks. In this case the rental income and even future capital growth may be of secondary importance. For others, however, who need the income and may be considering several purchases, the situation is more complicated and not without risks.

Holiday letting is very different from long-term letting. When a long-term tenant is in place the matter is usually settled and, in most cases, secure for three years or more (see Chapter 19). The rent is known in advance and will generally be inflation proofed. The tenant pays the bills. Apart from the cost of essential repairs (see Chapter 15), the landlord's financial commitment will be limited to his mortgage costs and income tax bills.

Holiday letting (*location saisonnière*), on the other hand, is more a *business* than a simple investment. Like any business it will be subject to risk and uncertainty. Some years will be better than others. Freak weather conditions, a natural disaster such as a volcanic eruption or an earthquake, a rail or air strike, a terrorist attack – each could have a devastating effect. Currency fluctuations or a recession could discourage people from holidaying abroad. Such events are beyond anyone's control and are inherently unpredictable.

BASIC QUESTIONS

While acts of God are unpredictable, it is possible to prepare for other more mundane risks by asking some obvious questions:

- How long is the season?

- What annual rent is achievable?

- What is the likely occupancy rate?

- Which districts are most popular?

- Which types of property let best?

- Is there oversupply?

With the exception of Paris (which is in year-round demand) holiday destinations will have a clearly defined season, outside of which no holiday letting at all will be possible. Rents may also be subject to variation during the season. By definition there will be no rents at all out of season. Then there is the matter of the occupancy rate which may differ considerably from one district to another and one type of property to another. Are some areas oversupplied? It is clearly essential to have answers to these questions before a final decision is made on a property purchase.

While local letting agents are a useful source of information regarding long-term letting (See Chapter 20), they are generally of little use when it comes to holiday letting. They tend to have limited experience in this area. Fortunately, it is not at all difficult to get this information elsewhere – on the web.

The only realistic way of letting a holiday property today is to advertise it on one of the dedicated sites for property owners (see Chapter 13). For each property advertised in this way the site provides details of the rent charged and an availability calendar for the potential tenant. If the rent varies throughout the season these details will be provided. The availability calendar will show the bookings already made for the coming weeks and months. The occupancy rate is there for all to see. At a glance, therefore, it is possible to gauge the popularity of certain areas and the rent that can be achieved for properties within them.

While the availability calendar is invaluable it does, however, have a drawback. At the beginning of each month the previous month, with all its data, is removed. While it is always possible to look ahead it is never possible to look back! For this reason these sites should be visited regularly, every month, for as long as possible before a search for a property is undertaken. This is also necessary to establish accurately the *length of the season*. Finally, why not talk to one or two owners? Their numbers are provided on the sites.

BUYING THE RIGHT PROPERTY

Having established that the location is in demand and occupancy rates high, it is necessary to decide on the *type* of property to buy – apartment, cottage, house or villa.

In many cases the location will make the decision for you. There will be few apartments in rural areas and no idyllic cottages along the *Promenade des Anglais* in Nice. Budget constraints will further limit the choice. A villa may be out of the question, as may a one-, two- or three-bedroom apartment. Buying a small studio may be the only option. Where there is a choice to be made, however, a few points are worth noting:

▪ A glance at the holiday letting websites (see above) will show that very high rents can be achieved for luxury villas (with very high price tags, of course). This market, however, is narrow and the occupancy rates for this type of property need to be carefully scrutinised in the availability calendars. In the event of a prolonged dip in occupancy the loss of income will be substantial. If this rental income is needed to service a very high mortgage the consequences could be dire. The sites will also show if there is much of a demand for high-end properties of this kind in the off-season.

▪ At the other end of the spectrum the relative rent levels and occupancy rates for apartments of various sizes need to be examined with care. Are three-bedroom apartments always in demand? Is the market for couples stronger than for groups? Is the extra cost of a large apartment justified, given the likely rent and the cost of servicing the mortgage? Which type of apartment seems to let best in the off-season?

DOING THE SUMS

At this point a tentative figure can be put on the annual rent achievable, while the price of the property and related mortgage costs will already be known. Is this now a viable investment? Are there financial risks ahead?

If a mortgage (UK or French) is to be used for the purchase the likely cost of this will be known in advance. While it is very tempting to focus on this figure when deciding on the viability or otherwise of the purchase (i.e. will the potential rent cover the mortgage?) it would be a mistake to do so.

What is missing here is the cost of the incidental, but entirely unavoidable, expenses which will follow the purchase of the property. These can seriously undermine the viability of the investment.

Incidental expenses

The number and the level of these can come as a shock. Here, as an example, is the list for a one-bedroom apartment in a typical *copropriété* or co-ownership building:

utilities

repairs/maintenance

insurance

copropriété *charges*

TV licence

cleaner

agent

advertising costs

taxe foncière

taxe d'habitation

income tax.

How to quantify these costs?

The answer, for most of these, is through the *selling agent*. The vendor, after all, has had the unpleasant experience of paying most of these bills – utilities, *copropriété* charges (see Chapter 7), TV licence, insurance, *Taxe Foncière* and *Taxe d'Habitation* (see Chapter 24). The agent should be asked to obtain these details from the vendor to cover at least the last 12-month period. The agent will also know the hourly rate for a cleaner in the area (typically €10–€15) and may be willing to recommend one. As both the agent and the vendor want to sell the property it can be expected that this information will be readily provided.

For repairs and maintenance allow 5% of annual rent. For advertising costs expect to pay £250–£300 per property (see Chapter 13). For income tax purposes assume the *micro-bic* regime (see Chapter 21) whereby 50% of the gross annual rent is taxed at a flat 20% (i.e. 10% of gross rent). If both a managing agent and a cleaner are required allow €100–€150 per letting.

Example

A one-bedroom apartment in the Old Town of Nice with a 16-week season and an anticipated annual income of €6,000.

utilities	420
copropriété	500
repairs	250
insurance	200
advertising	250
cleaner/agent	130
taxe foncière	300
taxe d'habitation	450
TV licence	120
income tax	600
	———
Total	3,220

An annual income of €6,000 in this case would cover the anticipated running costs, leaving €2,780 to go towards the cost of any mortgage taken out to buy the property.

As some of these 'incidental' costs can differ greatly from one area (and one building) to another it is crucial to factor them in before any decision is made to purchase. In the case, for example, of an apartment building with a lift and a swimming pool, the *copropriété* charges would be very much greater than the figure in the above example. Yet the rent achievable may not be much more.

THE RIGHT INSURANCE

Once the property is bought it must be insured. Cover for a holiday let property, however, needs to be chosen with care. The wrong insurance can mean no cover at all. See Chapter 10.

13

Getting Started

Having chosen the location, calculated the risk and made the purchase, it is time to get the business under way.

At the outset, it is crucial to be aware of and comply with the legal framework for holiday letting in France.

With the legal niceties out of the way it is time to decide how the business will be run. Should you hand the whole management over to an agency or do it yourself? If direct involvement is the choice some initial groundwork is required. The property will need to be cleaned and the sheets laundered between stays. A cleaner must be hired. It may also be very useful to have someone local who can deal with queries from guests and handle repairs or emergencies if required. The rent level needs to be chosen. Then the property must be furnished and prepared for its new role. Finally, steps must be taken to find the all-important tenants.

FRENCH REGULATIONS

Compared to the highly restrictive legislation in place for long-term letting (see Chapter 15), the rules governing holiday letting are considerably more relaxed. So long as the rental period for a tenancy is no more than 90 days (generally accepted as the upper limit for a holiday let) and so long as the property will not be the tenant's principal residence, the tenancy does not come under the 1989 legislation on rental accommodation (see Chapter 15). Instead, it is subject to article 1708 of the Civil Code. Consequently, there are no restrictions on the rent that can be charged and no issues regarding security of tenure for the tenant.

At the same time the owner is expected to provide, in writing, a full description of the property, its precise location, the rent and other charges applicable (article L324-2 of the *Code du Tourisme*), along with other essential details such as the deposit required, the dates of arrival and departure etc.

The deposit

French holidaymakers renting a property in France will expect the deposit to be described as either *arrhes* or *acompte*. The distinction is significant. If it is an *arrhes* and the client cancels his booking, he will lose his deposit. If the owner cancels the booking, however, he will have to pay his would-be client *double* the deposit paid (article 1590 of the Civil Code). In the case of an *acompte* either party would have to compensate the other fully for a cancellation. The tenant would not only lose his deposit, he would have to pay the full cost of the rental. The owner would have to make full financial redress to the tenant for the cancelled holiday.

Registration

Like most countries, France has a system of registration for holiday lettings. From 1 July 2010 it is a *legal requirement* to register a holiday let property (apartment, *villa, gîte* or other) at the local Town Hall (*mairie*) before any holiday letting takes place (article L324-1-1 of the *Code du Tourisme*). Cerfa form 14004-01 can be obtained from the Town Hall or downloaded from the net. Failure to register will incur a fine under article R 324-1-2 of the *Code du Tourisme*.

Paris alert!

Paris has its own rules regarding holiday lets. Registration alone will not suffice. If the intended rental period is less than 12 months (or nine months in the case of a student let) an application for change of use (from residential to commercial) must be lodged with the *Mairie*. A permit will only be granted for the holiday let if the applicant can also provide *another* property of similar size and in a similar location which can be let long term at an affordable rent. Clearly impossible in most cases. In this way it is hoped more affordable long-term accommodation will become available for Parisians.

While the rules have existed for some time they have not been enforced and have largely been ignored. Early in 2010, however, the mayor of Paris announced that he had every intention of enforcing them. A successful prosecution for breaking the law could result in a substantial fine and a criminal record. Given the consternation that met the mayor's announcement, however, it is possible that this situation could change in the future. In the meantime legal advice from a good Parisian *notaire* is essential before embarking on a holiday let purchase in Paris.

Tourist classification

Gîte owners have long been able to gain a special certification from the national organisation for *gîtes* owners – *Gîtes de France*. Under this system each *gîte* is awarded 1, 2, 3, 4 or 5 ears of corn (*épis*), depending on amenities, location etc. Owners of other holiday let properties, however (apartments, studios, villas) can also have their own certification as *meublés de tourisme* if they wish to apply for it.

This is an *étoile* (star) classification, based on the amenities provided – from the simple and basic to the luxurious. Applications are made through the local Town Hall (*mairie*). Visits are arranged by the *préfecture*, reports passed to the *mairie* and a classification (1–5 stars) duly awarded. Application forms are available from the local *mairie*.

There is a clear marketing advantage in acquiring a good star classification. But it does not come without responsibilities. Each star rating demands minimum standards which must be maintained. The property is subject to reinspection every five years. There is also a formal complaints procedure for tenants who can complain to the *Comité Départemental du Tourisme*.

AGENCIES OR DIY

It is perfectly possible to delegate everything to an outside agency and have no involvement at all in the day-to-day running of the business. The alternative is to be fully involved. Surprisingly, there is no viable middle course.

There are agencies which will happily take the property off your hands and manage everything for you (see Appendix C) – provided it is the sort of property they are looking for and, crucially, is in the right location. After an initial inspection they will offer suggestions regarding the facilities etc. they will expect to be provided, indicate the market they would expect to target (couples, groups etc.) and the rent they would expect to get.

Full management will involve advertising the property on the agency's website, taking bookings and deposits, providing linen and towels, doing the laundry, attending to repairs, collecting clients from the airport if required and handling any queries during their clients' stay. The agency pays the owner by bank transfer on a monthly basis and provides him with regular booking schedules. When he wishes to stay at the property himself he stays as a 'guest' of the agency, free of charge. At the end of the year he is provided with an annual statement for tax purposes.

Such a comprehensive service is clearly attractive but it comes with two serious drawbacks:

- The agreement with the owner will normally be in the form of an *exclusive* contract for a set term (e.g. 12 months). During this time it will not be possible to market the property privately or use other agencies. It is very unlikely that a single agency will generate enough business on its own. If the bookings do not materialise there is nothing the owner can do.

- The cost of this service may prove prohibitive. As much as two thirds of the rental income can disappear in agency fees. Yet the running costs of the property (see Chapter 12) have still to be met. Covering costs will be very difficult, making a profit almost certainly impossible.

Realistically, the only way to make a holiday letting investment pay is for the owner to do as much of the work as possible. Essentially, this involves marketing the property, fielding enquiries, taking bookings, accepting payment and arranging cleaning, laundry and general maintenance.

This may sound daunting and time consuming but once the initial groundwork is completed the operation is perfectly manageable and restricted, in most cases, to three or four months of the year.

CLEANER/AGENT

Finding a cleaner is not difficult but finding a good, reliable one is another matter. A recommendation is clearly desirable. The first place to enquire is the estate agency through which the property was bought. They may know someone looking for this work. If the property is an apartment the concierge of the building may be able to recommend someone. Failing that, the concierge of the building next door might be able to help. If language is an issue ask at the nearest Irish pub! At all costs avoid the specialist cleaning agencies. They will charge more than double the going rate and you will have no direct contact with the cleaners.

On the internet *craigslist, angloInfo, franglo* and *justlanded* are useful sources of English speakers looking for work (see Appendix C). An advert looking for a cleaner can also be placed on these sites. If language is not an issue a search for *femme de ménage* (housekeeper) in the small ads (*petites annonces*) of the website *vivastreet* (see Appendix C) will also produce results.

As bookings can often be back-to-back (a tenant leaving in the morning and another arriving in the afternoon) the cleaner's role is critical. She must be available when required and have a reliable substitute if, for any reason, she can't make it. She will be expected to manage the stock of linen and towels, providing fresh ones for each new tenant. She might choose to wash and iron at home or take the sheets, quilt covers, pillowslips and towels to a nearby laundry (*blanchisserie*) for collection again on her return visit. A cleaner would expect to earn €10–€15 per hour plus the laundry bill.

In addition to a cleaner it is advisable to have someone available locally to handle any problems that may arise and check the property for damage (in some cases the cleaner may be willing and able to fill this role). The best way to find such a person is through local lettings and sales agents. While they are unlikely to be in this market themselves they are well placed to know someone who is. Some ex-pats in tourist areas make a living by managing properties in this way for British and American investors. They make themselves known to local estate agents and advertise their services on websites such as *craigslist* (see above). While the going rate for a cleaner is easily established there is no set rate for a 'managing agent' of this sort.

RENT AND OTHER CHARGES

However wonderful your property may be, for most people price is a crucial factor. A like-for-like comparison must be made with properties offering similar facilities, in the same location and aimed at the same market (families, couples etc.). Such a comparison is simple to make as details of competing properties are conveniently displayed on the holiday letting websites (see below).

A glance at these sites will also show that rents usually vary from one part of the season to another. People expect to pay more in the high season, for example, than they would in April or May. Mid-term breaks in UK schools produce their own increase in demand for these dates, leading to higher rents. Check also if discounts are being offered for last minute bookings and whether special deals are on offer for short breaks or longer lettings in the off-season.

In addition to the rent a refundable damage deposit is routinely required and the level of this needs to be considered carefully.

A very high deposit can put people off. Some will worry about how much of it is at risk and how difficult it may be to get it back. While a substantial deposit may be a sensible requirement when large groups or children and pets are involved, it might well deter a couple planning to rent a small studio.

The question of utility bills needs to be considered when setting the rent. Charging separately for these may make it possible to set a lower headline rent and thus attract more interest. On the other hand, meters need to be read before and after the letting and there is always the risk of disputes. Tenants undoubtedly prefer the simplicity of an inclusive price. However, this invariably makes for higher bills as there is no incentive to economise.

A similar issue arises when it comes to the laundry bill and the fees for the cleaner and agent. Including these in the rent is a simple solution but this may make the property seem expensive compared to others where they are listed as an extra charge. It also means that the cleaner has to wait for payment. In many cases the decision on this matter is taken out of the owner's hands as cleaners and agents much prefer to be paid in cash (*en espèces*). The only practical way to achieve this is for the client to leave the fee, in cash, in the property at the end of his stay.

PREPARING THE PROPERTY

It is important to bear in mind that it is a holiday home, not a permanent home, that will be rented out – a stay of just a week will be typical. With the exception of the luxury villa market, tenants will be looking for functionality rather than luxury. The rustic charm of a country cottage or the ancient staircases of buildings in the Old Town of Nice are features rather than drawbacks. It is not, therefore, necessary to spend large sums on expensive furniture or state-of-the-art equipment. Holidaymakers will not expect them.

Furniture should be functional. Instead of a sofa in the lounge, for example, think of the extra sleeping space a sofa-bed (*canapé*) would provide. If space is at a premium folding chairs and a folding table are perfectly acceptable to holiday tenants. If children are accepted a high chair is an important item of furniture. Where decor is concerned, don't worry too much about neutral colours and all the other things that are relevant for long-term tenants. People on holiday know that this is your home, not theirs, and expect to find your own stamp on the property.

A well-equipped kitchen is very important. Apart from a fridge-freezer there should be a microwave, at least two hot plates or *plaques électriques* (a full conventional oven is not necessary), a toaster (essential for the British) and a coffee percolator (essential for Americans). A dishwasher is an attractive add-on, but not essential. If there is room for a washing machine, however, this should be installed. Although few short-stay holidaymakers will use it, it will be a definite requirement for any medium-stay tenant (see below). Needless to say, there should be adequate supplies of crockery and cutlery.

As for the bathroom (*salle de bains*) a shower, rather than a bath, is the top priority for most holidaymakers. For this reason the absence of a bath will not pose a problem. A shower room (*salle d'eau*) will be quite acceptable. Where there is no window a strong extractor fan (*ventilateur*), in good working order, is essential.

Holidaymakers will expect to find a hairdryer, an iron and an ironing board. If the property is near a beach they will be pleasantly surprised to find a few beach-mats or lilos.

Air conditioning (*climatisation*) is clearly a desirable feature in the warmer parts of the country but, perhaps surprisingly, is not usually a deal breaker. The rent, the property and the location will usually be the deciding factors. Having said that, however, there is no getting away from the extreme heat that can sometimes sweep across the south of the country. Electric fans are essential, both in the living areas and the bedrooms (one on each side of the bed!). Installing air conditioning is always possible, but it should be noted that this will cause a major hike in utility bills as tenants can be relied upon to leave it on, on full power, 24 hours a day. Air conditioning salesmen will point out that modern A/C systems will also produce heat very cheaply in the winter. However, this is when the property will most likely be empty! When considering installing A/C in an apartment remember that permission will be needed from the *syndic* or management committee (see Chapter 7).

A TV, DVD player and CD player are basic requirements. Consideration should also be given to cable TV so that English channels are available. For short-term holidaymakers this is not a serious issue but it can be important for others. The same is true of internet access. For most tenants internet cafes and WiFi hot spots are sufficient. For the tenant staying three or four weeks or a few months, however, internet access in the property is a definite plus. A cheap solution is to subscribe to a cable TV and internet package offered by companies such as *Numericable* (see Appendix C). A telephone line may be a requirement in this case. If so, care needs to be taken to ensure that calls can be received but not made.

The cleaner will expect to find at least three sets of quilt covers, sheets (preferably fitted sheets), pillowcases, towels (large and small) and tea towels. As tenants will use whatever is left lying around she will need a lockable box or cupboard to store linen that is not required. A vacuum cleaner is a must.

With an eye to safety the property should be thoroughly checked for avoidable risks. Particular care needs to be taken if children are to be accepted. Can the windows be reached by a toddler? Could a child lock himself in the bathroom?

How safe is the pool? There are very strict regulations regarding swimming pools in France. In compliance with the law of 3 January 2003 all pools must have an alarm system, a safety cover and a protective barrier. Failure to comply with this law is not only an offence in itself it will invalidate the swimming pool cover provided by any insurance policy (see Chapter 10).

An electrical safety check should be carried out and the documentation relating to this carefully filed. If children are accepted a stair gate should be provided. A first aid kit should be to hand and emergency numbers prominently displayed.

Holidaymakers will be pleased to find information about the area when they check in to the property. The local tourist office will provide leaflets and brochures on festivals, major events and must-see attractions. These should be collected from time to time and made available in the property. Directions to the tourist office will be welcomed.

It is always helpful to put up notices in the property about really important matters such as emergency numbers, a reminder about the check-out time, arrangements for rubbish collection or the phone number for your agent in case of problems. These notices should be short and to the point, carefully printed (not hand written) and laminated for long-term use (any local newsagent will laminate).

Tips

Provide a Guest Book for holidaymakers' comments and suggestions. New arrivals find this very helpful.

Ask the cleaner to leave a welcoming card and a bottle of wine for the next guest.

Leave a key to the property with a neighbour. In the event of an emergency, such as a flood in an apartment building, this could mean the difference between an awkward incident and a total catastrophe. In the case of an apartment building it is the neighbour downstairs who will most willingly take on this responsibility!

TENANTS FROM THE WEB

There is only one reliable way to secure holiday letting tenants – the internet. Word of mouth, local adverts, friends, colleagues, adverts in property magazines (whatever they tell you) will never achieve the level of enquiries required to fill your vacant slots.

Holidaymakers, considering self-catering accommodation, will do one thing only – search the web. This invariably takes the form of a general search (typically a Google search) using such phrases as *Holiday apartment Paris* or *Cottage in the Dordogne*. The result is hundreds of pages of potential providers of accommodation. But only one page really matters – page one. Nobody bothers with the rest.

To see how this works Google search a holiday let in your area. What you see on page one is where you have to be. How do you get there? The answer is to hitch a ride on one or more of the websites specialising in holiday lets for private owners. Only those sites that always appear on page one should be considered. See *Holiday let websites for owners* in Appendix C for the most successful sites.

The principle is simple. In return for an annual fee the site will advertise your property, complete with text and photos, and pass on any enquiries, by email, to you (an SMS text alert option is usually available). You then deal directly with the client. It is a simple matter to add your property to the site. Instructions are provided for uploading photos and text, filling in an availability calendar and listing facilities offered. There is a section for local activities such as golf, tennis and skiing and another for transport links, including distance from the airport and railway station. Some sites provide a Google map which will pinpoint the property's exact location. You will be asked to state whether you will accept children or pets and whether the property is suitable for the elderly or infirm. In the rental section you choose the rent you wish to charge and the currency you will accept. Various rent levels for different times of the year (and nightly or weekly rates) can be accommodated. When you have completed the advertisement you pay the fee online. The property should be live on the site within 48 hours.

Text and photos

The photographs are by far the most important part of the advert. It is these, not the text, that will draw the reader's attention (between four and 16 photos are allowed, depending on the site). Great care needs to be taken with them.

Make sure there is plenty of light when taking the photos. Add warmth and colour by using a vase of flowers, a table lamp and prints on the walls. Avoid clutter.

Readers will expect to see the living area, bedrooms, kitchen and bathroom. If one of these is missing they will wonder why. They will also like to see something of the surrounding area such as the beach, local street scenes, the market etc. These scenes, captured on camera, can be just as important in swaying viewers' decisions as photos of the property itself.

Local activities (swimming, golf, skiing etc.) and tourist attractions should be comprehensively listed in the general description of the area. Next on the list for most holidaymakers will be food. Clients will want to know about local dishes, recommended restaurants and food markets. Leave nothing out.

Most sites allow for additional notes on the rent charged. Here you can list any extra charges (e.g. for cleaning), specify the deposit required on booking and any damage deposit to be charged. The payment options (credit card, PayPal etc.) could also be highlighted here.

Link to own website

A useful option in most advertising sites is a link to the customer's own website. This can be free of charge if it is reciprocal (i.e. a link also provided from the customer's site to the advertiser's site). If it is not reciprocal there will be an extra charge (typically £30).

In terms of securing business a private website is of little use as it will never feature on page one of a Google search. It is very useful, however, as a vehicle for additional information and photos not featured in the advertising site. The link sends the potential client directly to the owner's site.

Customer reviews

A few sites allow holidaymakers to post a review of the property at the end of their stay. There is no doubt that a glowing review is very welcome and can attract more business but the review system as a whole is a mixed blessing. With the best will in the world things can go wrong. A highly critical review can put an end to any further business from that site. In addition it is not unknown for a canny holidaymaker to make full use of this situation and drop broad hints that a full or partial refund might discourage him from posting his review!

Position in the search results

The success of these sites (always on page one of a Google search) has one disadvantage – the sheer number of properties they carry. Your property will have to compete with many others on page after page of similar properties on the site. Will people have the patience to find yours?

This problem is recognised by the largest sites. The solution they have come up with is to adjust the position of a property (i.e. the page on which it appears) according to the *activity of the owner* on the site. At any time an owner can make alterations to his advert, usually by adjusting the availability calendar. This can take the form of adding a booking or simply marking some dates available. Every time this happens the property moves up the pecking order. Regular changes of this kind can keep a property in the first half dozen pages. Conversely, persistent inactivity will consign the property to oblivion.

Scams

There are inherent risks for anyone using the internet but property owners using these sites need to be particularly vigilant. There are two dangers to watch out for – bogus bookings and phishing.

The bogus booking involves making the rental payment by cheque, but for considerably more than is required. The owner is then asked to rectify this 'oversight' by refunding the balance – but not by cheque. Having made the refund, perhaps by bank transfer, the property owner is unaware that the original cheque is still working its way through the clearing system and is about to bounce!

In the case of phishing it is the property owner's clients who could suffer. In this case the fraudster gains access to the owner's username and password by providing a link to a bogus, but plausible, website. Armed with this information he can access the owner's email account and invoice his clients for the rent!

Cost

Expect to pay between £150 and £300 a year + VAT for a listing. It is possible to choose a six-month listing but this is discouraged by charging only slightly less than the annual fee for it. Some sites offer a discount for listing more than one property and some charge extra for each photo above a certain number. There are sites which don't charge a fee at all but take a commission on the rent for any bookings made through the site – typically 10%. Unless there are very few bookings, however, this will normally be a much more expensive option.

MEDIUM-TERM TENANTS

There is a steady rental market which is neither holiday let nor long-term – typically three to six months in the off-season. The demand mainly comes from house hunters, students on languages courses, academics on sabbatical and retirees. It can be a very useful way of bridging the rental gap which otherwise is unavoidable.

The good news is that the sites which advertise holiday lets also attract these enquiries. In addition, there are a few sites which specialise in this market (see Appendix C).

This is an area, however, of some legal complexity and care needs to be taken. As we shall see (Chapters 6–8) long-term letting is very strictly regulated indeed. What the holiday let owner does not want to find is that his 'medium-term' tenant has become a 'long-term' tenant overnight!

To avoid falling foul of French law it is essential to know if the tenancy in question is covered by past and current legislation. There is a simple test to establish this:

Will the property be the tenant's principal residence?

The 1989 Act and subsequent legislation (see Chapters 15–17) only apply if the property, furnished or unfurnished, is to be the tenant's main residence. In the case of a typical holiday let of one or two weeks this would clearly not be the case. In other cases, however, such as those listed above, it may not be so obvious. While the tenant on sabbatical has clearly got a home to go to the house hunter may already have disposed of his home. In this case the rented property will be his main home and the full rigour of the law will apply – with all that this implies for minimum contract terms, tenant security, notice periods, deposits etc. (see Chapters 15–17). The prospective tenant should be asked to declare his position in this regard and to make this declaration in writing. Where there is any doubt the only safe course is to consult a *notaire* before proceeding with the letting.

14

Day-to-Day Management

As with any business, marketing is only part of the story. Once the enquiries come in the business needs to be promptly secured and tied down. A booking contract must be prepared. Options for payment methods need to be decided on and payment received. Provision for key collection must be put in place. General information, instructions and directions have to be given to the holidaymaker well in advance. The cleaner and agent need to be kept up to date with bookings and a decision made with them regarding check-in and check-out times. As things can become quite hectic when the season begins systems need to be in place to ensure that mistakes are not made.

SECURING THE BUSINESS

There is plenty of evidence from research carried out by holiday rental sites that speed of response is the single most important factor in securing bookings. There is so much competition and such a wide choice that a delay of 24 hours can easily lose the business. While it is not possible to remain glued to the computer at all times there is a simple way of knowing that an enquiry has come in – an SMS text alert. This is an option available from most sites at no extra cost. To speed up the process of dealing with enquiries it is advisable to have standard texts saved to the computer's desktop. These can be copied and pasted, as needed, to an email. There could be one for responding to an initial enquiry, one to confirm a booking, one acknowledging payment etc.

After speed of response comes *trust*. The holidaymaker is not dealing with a large established company and initially may be nervous about renting a property in this way. What if that lovely apartment in Cannes turns out to be a Chinese restaurant with a very angry proprietor? It is essential to establish quickly that you exist outside of cyberspace and that you have a real physical address. An initial phone call from a landline (not a mobile) is a good beginning. Apart from acknowledging receipt of payment by email a formal receipt with a compliment slip and business card (with name, address and contact details) should be posted to the client. This helps to reassure the holidaymaker that he is dealing with a professional, well-organised business. Money spent on good quality stationery is very well spent.

BOOKING CONTRACT AND BOOKING TERMS

The booking contract legally seals the deal and, as such, is a crucial document. The booking terms set out the conditions which the prospective tenant must accept. These can be incorporated in the contract itself or presented as a separate document. Whatever the format, the following points should be covered:

Parties to the agreement

The name and address of both the owner and the tenant should appear. Where there is more than one tenant all names should be listed. Where there is a 'no children' policy or where the premises are not suitable for the elderly it is advisable to ask for confirmation of the tenants' respective ages. Asking someone's age, however, can be a delicate matter. The solution is to ask the client to choose from a list of age ranges : 20–30, 30–40 etc.

The property

Full address of the rental property including, where relevant, apartment number and floor.

Booking confirmation

The fact that a booking is requested does not mean that it will inevitably go ahead. The conditions for confirmation should be set out. These will normally include the return of the signed contract with the initial payment and confirmation in writing by the owner that the booking is accepted.

Dates

To avoid confusion the dates of the tenancy should be in the format: 'arrival date . . . departure date . . . '.

Check-in/check-out times

This is a matter of great importance in the high season (see below). The tenant needs to be reminded that these times are not vague guidelines.

Number of occupants

It will already be clear how many intend to stay in the property. It is worth mentioning separately, however, that this figure is the maximum allowable. It is not unknown for holidaymakers to pay scant regard to this. Four people sharing a studio intended for two will have a very cheap holiday and leave a great deal of work for the cleaner.

Pets/children/smoking

Where pets and children are specifically excluded it is important to refer to this directly. The same applies if smoking is not allowed. The client must confirm acceptance of these terms.

Rent and other charges

The full rent payable should be clearly stated plus any additional charges (e.g. cleaning or utilities) if applicable.

Payment options

Payment methods accepted (cheque, credit card, PayPal etc.) should be stated here. Where the client has already chosen a method this should be indicated. If there are additional costs involved in some payment methods it should be made clear what these are and who is expected to pay them. Bank transfers, for example, from outside the EU frequently incur bank charges. Likewise, if you offer credit card facilities you may wish to charge a 'handling fee'.

Initial payment and balance

Except for last-minute bookings full payment would not normally be required at the time of booking. An initial payment, with the balance to be paid at a later date, is the standard procedure. The amount of the initial payment, the balance and the date the balance is due should all be specified.

Security deposit

A separate refundable deposit is always required to cover the cost of any damage that may be caused to the property. It can also be used to cover other eventualities such as the loss of keys, leaving the property in a particularly dirty condition, compensation for exceeding the maximum number of occupants etc. The level of the deposit required and the circumstances in which it might be retained, in whole or in part, should be clearly specified in the contract. The timescale envisaged for the refund of the deposit should also be indicated.

Cancellation

The cancellation policy is a vital part of the contract. If he cancels the booking, the tenant needs to understand when and under what circumstances he may lose some or all of the payment he has made. This is an area of particular concern to most holiday-makers and may influence their decision on whether to proceed with the booking. A typical formula will allow for a 50% refund if the cancellation is made between eight and four weeks before arrival and no refund if later than that.

There should be a reminder at this point that holiday insurance covers the more common reasons for cancellation and that such insurance is strongly recommended.

Disturbance/nuisance

Your tenants will need reminding that they have an obligation not to upset the neighbours or other occupants of the building.

Owner's liability

The limit to the owner's liability should be clearly set out. He will typically decline to take responsibility for costs incurred due to cancellation by the holidaymaker. The traveller should again be reminded to take out comprehensive insurance.

Acceptance of booking terms

Whether or not the booking terms are incorporated in the contract the client must confirm acceptance of these conditions. As the legal age for contractual liability is 18 he should also confirm that he is over 18.

Legal jurisdiction

In the event of a dispute the parties to the contract could end up in court. But which legal jurisdiction should apply? The contract should state that it is the law and legal system of England and Wales that will apply in such cases.

For an example of a booking contract and booking terms, see Appendix A.

PAYMENT OPTIONS

At some point money changes hands. How is the client to pay? There is a clear advantage in being able to offer all possible payment options – debit and credit card facilities, payments through PayPal as well as cheques and bank transfers.

PayPal, credit and debit card

While payments by cheque and bank transfer are routinely available many holidaymakers are more comfortable with plastic and would prefer to pay this way. To receive payment by credit card or debit card it is necessary to open a merchant account through a bank (satisfying all the bank's requirements for this) or use the merchant account of a third party such as PayPal (see Appendix C). In this case all that is required is to open a PayPal account, a relatively simple procedure. Once the account is up and running payments can be made to the account, using all major credit cards, debit cards or via the client's PayPal account. All that is needed is an email address to which an invoice or 'payment request' can be sent. The client does not need to have a PayPal account to make the payment. The transaction is instant and the payment credited immediately to the recipient's PayPal account (from which transfers can be made to a bank account whenever required).

If PayPal considers a payment to be suspect (perhaps from a stolen credit card) it will issue a warning to the account holder and conduct an investigation. Only when they are happy that all is satisfactory will the account holder be advised to proceed with the transaction.

All this comes at a price, of course. While there are no set-up fees and no monthly charge there is a charge levied on each transaction. The level of this charge varies with the volume of business transacted but 4% at least should be anticipated.

While credit card payments are very convenient it is worth noting that they can be subject to a 'chargeback'. This means that the customer can demand his money back if goods or services bought are faulty or never materialise. There is a period of 120 days in which to make a claim.

Tips

For security reasons make regular withdrawals from a PayPal account, leaving only the minimum needed for day-to-day transactions.

KEYS

In an ideal world clients would be met on arrival by the owner or his agent, welcomed to the property and presented with the keys. In reality a 'Meet and Greet' arrangement of this sort is rarely practical. For all sorts of reasons – flight delays, poor bus service from the airport, traffic hold-ups – a precise arrival time at the property is impossible to determine. Unless, therefore, the owner lives nearby or the agent has a great deal of time on his hands the only solution is for the holidaymaker to collect the keys locally on arrival or be in possession of the keys before arrival.

Key collection point

One solution is a local key collection point. This will typically be a nearby business (perhaps a shop, restaurant or pub) whose proprietor is happy to hold keys in return for a small consideration. A few important points to bear in mind about this arrangement:

- The business should be open until late (ideally until midnight), seven days a week.

- Security is a crucial issue. The keys should have no address on the tag and should be placed in an envelope with the name of the client only on the front. No address. Holidaymakers must be warned not to ask the staff for directions to the property.

Key safe

An alternative to a collection point is a Key Safe. This is simply a small lockable container holding the keys, mounted on an external wall near the door. They come either with a four-digit combination lock or a push-button code and can be bought on the internet or from DIY stores (price range typically £15–£35). They are not practical, however, for apartments as it is doubtful if the *Syndic* (management committee) would allow one to be mounted by the door to the building.

Post

If keys cannot be collected locally they can be posted to clients in advance, to be posted back on their return. This allows for the greatest flexibility in terms of arrival times and enables the holidaymakers to go directly to the property. Care needs to be taken, however, to get confirmation that the address is correct and to post the keys well in advance. For security reasons the address of the property should not be enclosed with the keys. As they may be slow to come back it is also important to have a sufficient number of keys cut to meet demand, especially in the high season. One drawback of this method is that it effectively rules out last-minute bookings.

INFORMATION FOR TENANTS

Prior to arrival the tenants should receive a full set of directions covering all modes of transport – air, rail and car. Bus connections from the airport are particularly important for the budget conscious traveller. Details provided should include the number of the bus, the number of the bus stand, the cost of the fare and where to get off. If there is more than one airport terminal two sets of instructions may be needed. In the case of Paris directions to the *RER* rail service from Charles de Gaulle airport and the bus service from Orly should be provided. For passengers arriving at Gare du Nord on the Eurostar an explanation of how to use the metro would be appreciated by the first-time visitor (how much are the tickets? What is a *carnet*? What does *correspondance* mean? etc.).

If keys have to be picked up directions to the pick-up point should be clear and precise. Other important information will include the opening hours of the business and instructions about asking for the keys (e.g. 'be polite to the staff! don't ask directions to the property' etc.). If a key safe is being used the tenant should be reminded to keep the code or combination lock numbers safe from prying eyes.

Other important reminders might include check-in and check-out times and any special arrangements regarding rubbish disposal. If using an agent make sure his contact number is provided.

INFORMATION FOR CLEANER/AGENT

When bookings are made on the net the cleaner and agent need to be kept informed via a regularly updated schedule of bookings (*planning*), emailed if possible. Apart from the arrival and departure dates the schedule should also indicate the approximate arrival times so that arrangements for key collection, where necessary, can be put in place in good time.

CHECK-IN/CHECK-OUT TIMES

It is the cleaner who must be considered here. There is nothing more certain to annoy her than holidaymakers arriving too early or failing to leave the property on time. In the high season, when many bookings can be back-to-back, this can have serious consequences. Once the check-in and check-out times have been agreed with the cleaner every effort should be made to ensure that the tenants comply with them (e.g. highlighted reminders prior to arrival and signs posted prominently in the property).

GOOD OFFICE PRACTICE

Once the bookings start to come in care needs to be taken to avoid some embarrassing and expensive mistakes:

- Double bookings.

- Keys not sent on time.

- Balance of rent due not requested.

- Deposits not refunded on time.

The consequences of a double booking don't bear thinking about. Apart from having to refund the rent there is the little matter of flights already booked and paid for and the cost of alternative accommodation. The aggrieved holidaymaker will expect full financial compensation. The safest thing to do is to adjust the availability calendar *immediately* after a booking is made, although payment will not have been received at this point and the booking contract will still be outstanding. With the dates on the calendar blanked out there is no risk of accepting another booking.

Enquiries for holiday accommodation will come from all over the world. Where keys have to be posted out in advance care needs to be taken to send them in plenty of time. It should also be noted that travellers from, say, Australia may leave home weeks before arriving at their holiday let property. Clients should routinely be asked if this is the case. Once a safe date for posting is established this should be entered in a PC or mobile phone calendar to provide a reminder when the due date arrives. Note also that keys can be sent 'Letter Post' or 'Small Packet'. Letter Post is always faster. A Post Book should be kept to record the dates keys, receipts and other correspondence are sent.

Most bookings require payment in two stages – an initial one at the time of booking and the balance at a specified date before arrival. Clients cannot be expected to remember the second payment and may miss it altogether if not reminded. One way to avoid this is to keep a separate 'Balance Due' schedule. This should list the client, the amount outstanding, the date due and the method of payment chosen. A glance at the schedule will tell who needs prompting.

Holidaymakers never forget that they have paid a damage deposit and take a dim view of any delay in refunding it. A week to ten days is generally considered a reasonable time in which to do so. It cannot, however, be returned until the cleaner has reported back on the state of the property. To that end a prompt to remind her should be entered in the calendar a few days after the end of each booking.

Part Four

LONG-TERM LETTING

Landlord's Rights and Obligations

For someone involved in the UK rental market the French system may come as a shock. In the UK the Assured Shorthold Tenancy (AST), introduced by the Housing Act 1988, completely transformed the rental scene. The tenant has the right to the property for the term of the tenancy (six or twelve months) and the landlord has the right to recover possession, easily and quickly, at the end of the tenancy. There is no permanent security of tenure for the tenant and the landlord needs no justification for taking possession at the end of the tenancy. There are few restrictions and obligations on landlord or tenant and the AST is the same for furnished and unfurnished lettings alike.

This simple state of affairs does not apply in France!

The French landlord and tenant scene for long-term rentals is possibly the most regulated in the world. There are rules about everything. The landlord and tenant legislation of 6 July 1989 established most of these rules and regulations and they are at the time of publication still in force. For the landlord they are particularly onerous. Failure to comply can lead to serious legal consequences.

TENANT REFERENCING

A landlord can reasonably expect his prospective tenant to have a monthly income equivalent to three or four times the monthly rent. To verify this he can ask for the following documentary evidence (*pièces justificatives*):

- Last three months' pay slips

- A copy of his contract of employment

- A reference from his current employer

- Confirmation of acceptance (in the case of a new job)

- Copy of a recent tax return (for self-employed or company directors)

- Revenue tax notice for the current tax year

- Receipts for the last payments to previous landlord.

Where a third party guarantee is required the guarantor can be asked for any or all of the above. In the case of a joint tenancy each prospective tenant may be asked for them.

There are some documents, however (since the *Loi de modernisation sociale* n°2002-73 of 17 January 2002), which the landlord is expressly *not* allowed to request – photographic ID, a bank reference, copy of a bank statement or social security card. As might be expected, he is also not allowed to discriminate on religious, sex, race or health grounds (*Code Pénal, articles 225-1 and 2*).

CONDITION OF THE PROPERTY

Under the *Loi Solidarité et Renouvellement Urbains* (SRU) of 14 December 2000 the landlord is obliged to provide his tenant with *un logement décent* or 'acceptable' accommodation. There should be nothing in the property that would pose a physical risk or constitute a health hazard for the tenant, whether the property is furnished or unfurnished. All normal facilities for day-to-day living should be provided and should be in good repair. Where repairs are required or where general wear and tear has reached an unacceptable level the landlord is obliged to put matters right. The tenant has recourse to the courts to enforce this obligation. The court can also reduce the rent.

Given the importance of these requirements, the inventory or *état des lieux* (which the landlord must provide at the beginning of the tenancy) takes on considerable significance. This is usually a very detailed document. It is checked, signed and dated by both parties, making it an *état des lieux contradictoire*. The tenant must be provided with a copy. At the end of the tenancy landlord and tenant go through the exercise again. If the property has not been left in good condition the landlord may withhold the deposit, or part of it, to pay for any work required to put matters right.

DEPOSIT

As in the UK there is no requirement for the landlord to ask for a deposit (*dépôt de garantie*) when letting a property but he is entitled to do so to protect himself against unpaid rent, damage to the property etc.

In the case of unfurnished letting the maximum deposit is one month's rent. There is no maximum for furnished lettings. Where rent is to be paid quarterly in advance (instead of monthly) no deposit at all can be demanded. There must be a clause in the contract referring specifically to the deposit and the amount. In the absence of such a clause no deposit can be required. Normally the deposit will be paid when the contract is signed. Where the deposit is to be paid later (after the tenancy has begun) this too must be detailed in the contract. The deposit cannot be increased during a tenancy or on renewal of a tenancy.

At the end of the tenancy, in the absence of any disagreement, the deposit must be repaid. The maximum time allowed for this is two months from the date the keys are returned (article 22 of the 6 July 1989 legislation). A delay beyond this will incur an interest charge on the amount outstanding.

Where damage has been done, rent or other charges unpaid, the landlord is entitled to retain all or part of the deposit to cover these costs. He must, however, produce the bills for the work done. Where his costs exceed the deposit he can demand a further payment from the tenant. If a dispute is unresolved it will end up in court. There is nothing in France comparable to the UK Tenancy Deposit Scheme which protects the tenant's deposit and provides a free arbitration service to resolve disputes.

REPAIRS

The landlord is responsible for essential repairs and general maintenance (*entretien*) of the property. A water heater (*ballon*), for example, will need descaling from time to time to maintain its efficiency. The tenant cannot be expected to do this. Likewise a central heating boiler (*chaudière*) will need to be serviced, repaired or even replaced if necessary. A faulty toilet cistern (*chasse d'eau*), a leaking radiator, a leaking roof would all fall to the landlord to repair. The tenant must allow reasonable access to carry out repairs and maintenance.

There can be areas, however, where disputes can arise. Normal wear and tear is considered reasonable for furniture and fittings, but at what point could the sofa be said to be in a state of dilapidation (*vétusté*) and in need of replacement, at the landlord's expense? On the other hand, a landlord could complain that his tenant's habit of drying his washing on the radiators and failing to open any windows has resulted in the rich crop of mould now working its way across the living room ceiling! A landlord or tenant responsibility?

Landlord's Notice

While a tenant can give notice at any time a landlord must allow the term of the tenancy to run its course. If he then wishes to recover possession he must give notice of either three months (furnished let) or six months (unfurnished) before the end of the tenancy. The notice must be in writing and sent by registered post with signed acknowledgement of receipt (*lettre recommandée avec accusé de reception*). It is from the date of this signature (not the date the letter was posted or the date of the notice itself) that the notice period (*délai de préavis*) runs. Alternatively, for a fee, the notice can be served by a court bailiff (*huissier de justice*).

The landlord, however, cannot recover his property simply because he has served the required notice. Unlike his UK counterpart, he must have a reason for repossession and only some reasons are acceptable. There are, in fact, only three reasons allowed by law – he needs the property for himself or his family, he wishes to sell or the tenant is in default.

The 'family' naturally includes husband and wife and civil partners but can also include a common-law spouse (*concubin/e*) so long as they were together for at least a year before serving the notice. Their close relatives (parents and children) are also included in the definition.

It is possible to sell a property during a tenancy but the tenancy cannot be interrupted. It must be sold tenanted with the new owner taking over the tenancy agreement. To sell unoccupied the owner must wait until the tenancy has run its course. In the case of an unfurnished tenancy, however, the landlord must give his tenant first refusal as the latter has a right of pre-emption enshrined in law (6 July 1989). To this effect he is obliged to serve his tenant with a notice of his intention to sell (*congé pour vente*). The notice must contain the price and conditions of sale, though it need not specify the dimensions of the property. The tenant has one month to respond. If he decides to buy he must complete the purchase in two months or, if he needs a mortgage, four months. If he fails to meet these deadlines he loses the property. If he decides not to buy he must vacate the property at the end of the tenancy.

Finally, notice can be served where a tenant is in clear breach of his contract. The most common reason is repeated delays in the payment of rent or other charges but it can also include unauthorised sub-letting (*sous-location*) causing damage to the property, failure to insure the property where that is the tenant's responsibility and causing a nuisance to neighbours. In this case it is clearly possible to end the tenancy before the end of the lease. But, where the tenant resists, the process can be long and arduous. The landlord's room for manoeuvre is severely limited if the transgressing tenant is over 70 by the end date of the tenancy agreement and is earning less than 1.5 × the minimum wage (*Salaire minimum interprofessionnel de croissance* or SMIC) when the notice is served. If both of these criteria are met he must find alternative accommodation for his tenant in the area! Only if the landlord himself is over 60 and also earning less than 1.5 × the minimum wage will he escape this requirement.

RENT INCREASE

It is possible to make the rent subject to an annual adjustment in line with the construction cost index (*Indice du Coût de la Construction* or ICC). This index is published by the *Institut national de la statistique et des études economiques* or INSEE. This can only happen, however, if there is a clause in the contract to this effect (for INSEE see *Rent increase* in Appendix C).

A wholesale revision of the rent, however, is another matter altogether and not easily achieved. In essence the landlord needs to establish that the rent currently paid is clearly below the rent regularly paid for similar properties in the same area (article 17 of the 6 July 1989 law). To this end he needs to gather evidence of rents paid over the last *three years* for similar properties in the same area (*loyers de référence*). This information is readily available through the *Union National de la Propriété Immobilière* (UNPI) which collects the data and makes it publicly available (see *Rent increase* in Appendix C).

An increase of this sort is possible only once every three years and then only at the end of a tenancy. A notice of at least six months is required (form 17c) before the end of the tenancy and the tenant must sign to acknowledge receipt. To establish his case the landlord must supply the tenant with three examples of rents paid locally for similar properties. If he is met with a deathly silence he can take the matter to the *Commission de Conciliation des Baux d'Habitation*. Should the tenant also ignore this or fail to attend the landlord cannot simply go ahead regardless. He must ask the *Tribunal d'instance* to authorise the increase.

COPROPRIETE CHARGES

When a landlord lets an apartment in a *copropriété* or co-ownership building (see Chapter 7) there are special circumstances to consider. For the most part the charges levied by the managing agency, are paid by the apartment owner. Some of these, however, are solely for the benefit of the tenant. The landlord has a right, in many cases, to recover these costs from the tenant.

Costs exclusively to be met by the landlord are the following: local property tax (*taxe foncière*), costs of major repairs and maintenance to the building and administrative costs levied by the managing agency or the *syndic*.

Other areas, however, are less clear-cut and costs are often shared between landlord and tenant. The tenant either pays the charges directly or the landlord recovers the cost, where appropriate, from the tenant. The following fit into this category:

■   Cost of annual mowing and maintenance of open spaces for common use are met by the tenant. The landlord, however, would foot the bill for replacing the flower beds, pruning or landscape gardening.

- The cost of hot and cold water is met by the tenant, though the portion relating to the caretaker's quarters would be met by the landlord.

- If the property needs to be disinfected (!) the tenant would share the cost of the products used but the landlord would pay the rest of the bill.

- Fuel bills and general maintenance for the heating system are solely the responsibility of the tenant. The landlord would be responsible for major repairs.

- The cost of insuring the building is shared by the landlord and the other copropriétaires (co-owners). The tenant is not involved.

- If there is a lift in the building it will need to be maintained and serviced. This is normally covered by a service contract, the cost of which is met by the tenant. If the contract is fully comprehensive and covers the possibility of major repairs and replacements the tenant is only responsible for 73% of the service contract cost and this is all the landlord can recover from him.

- A TV in the apartment requires an aerial or the installation of cable TV. This is the landlord's responsibility. The tenant, however, pays for the maintenance of the aerial and equipment.

- Major cleaning, repairing and painting in the common parts of the building are the landlord's responsibility. Routine cleaning of the common areas must be paid for by the tenant.

- Where there is a local tax for rubbish removal the tenant bears the cost.

ENERGY PERFORMANCE RATING

Since 1 July 2007 French landlords have been obliged to obtain an energy performance certificate or *diagnostic immobilier de performance énergétique* (DPE) and make it available to a prospective tenant *before* a contract is signed.

The purpose of the DPE (equivalent to the EPC or Energy Performance Certificate in the UK) is to enable tenants to compare rental properties for their energy use. The property is given a certificate or label (*étiquette*) for the energy efficiency of the property and another for its greenhouse effect (*à effet de serre*). Ratings range from A to G. The work must be carried out by specially trained assessors who comply with articles L.271-4 to L.271-6 of the *Code de la Construction et de l'Habitation*. Estate agents and *notaires* have lists of assessors as have the local offices of the *Agence de l'Environnement et de la Maîtrise de l'Energie* (ADEME). The certificates are valid for ten years.

16

Tenant's Rights and Obligations

Apart from having a general right to a *logement décent* (provided by the 6 July 1989 Act) and the right not to be discriminated against on religious, sex, race or health grounds (enshrined in articles 225-1 and 2 of the Penal Code) the French tenant enjoys a number of specific, legally enforceable, rights and privileges.

CONTRACT TERM AND SECURITY

The tenant has a right to a minimum term of one year (furnished) or three years (unfurnished). During this time he has total security of tenure. The property can be sold during the tenancy but in this case it must be sold let (*loué*), with the tenant and tenancy agreement undisturbed.

Even at the end of the contract the tenant has a right to a new contract unless the landlord can show that he needs the property for himself or his family, he wishes to sell or the tenant is in default.

TENANT'S NOTICE

Only the landlord is legally committed to the contract for its duration. The tenant can leave when he likes provided he gives the correct notice (one month for furnished or three months for unfurnished). Even here allowances are made for a tenant in difficult circumstances. If he is starting a new job, being transferred, is in poor health, is over 60 or is on income support (RMI or *revenu minimum d'insertion*) he need give only one month's notice where three would otherwise be required.

RIGHTS OF THE ELDERLY TENANT

If the tenant is in breach of contract but is over 70 by the end date of the tenancy agreement and is earning less than 1.5 × the minimum wage (*salaire minimum interprofessionnel de croissance* or SMIC) the landlord cannot serve notice without first finding alternative accommodation for his tenant.

RENT INCREASES

When it comes to rent increases the tenant enjoys a considerable degree of protection. If there is no clause in the contract referring to future increases he can legally refuse to accept one. Where an increase is allowed it cannot exceed the annual Cost of Construction Index (*Indice du Coût de la Construction*). A major increase in rent above this is only possible once in three years and then only if the landlord can prove the current rent is out of line with rents for comparable properties locally. If the tenant objects the whole matter must go to arbitration.

DEPOSIT

The tenant can be asked for a deposit but this is restricted by law to one month's rent (for an unfurnished let). If he pays quarterly in advance he does not have to provide a deposit at all. He is entitled to have the deposit refunded within two months of returning the keys.

CHOICE OF INSURANCE COMPANY

While a tenant must insure an unfurnished property (see below) he reserves the right to choose his own insurance company for this purpose. The landlord cannot insist on a company of his choosing.

RIGHT OF PRE-EMPTION

If the landlord decides to sell the property at the end of the tenancy his tenant has a legal right of pre-emption, i.e. first refusal.

RIGHT TO ARBITRATION

In the event of a dispute with the landlord (over rent, charges deposit etc.) the tenant can take the matter to the local *Commission des Recours Locatifs*. This is an arbitration service, established by the 6 July 1989 Act, to deal with landlord and tenant issues and avoid, where possible, the need for litigation.

Articles 7a to 7g of the 6 July 1989 Act set out the principal *obligations* imposed on the tenant.

PAYMENT OF RENT

The most important obligation (Article 7a) is the duty to pay the rent and charges as and when required by the terms of the contract. In most cases this will be monthly in advance. The contract can be terminated if the tenant fails to do this.

USE OF PROPERTY

The tenant must use the property 'peacefully' and only for the purpose intended (Article 7b). Playing loud music and annoying the neighbours would be a clear breach of contract. When the contract states that the property is for residential use only the tenant cannot run a business there without getting written permission from the landlord (and then registering the business at the local *registre du commerce*).

LIABILITY FOR DAMAGE

Liability for any damage or loss caused during the tenancy (Article 7c) rests solely with the tenant unless he can show that it was caused by a third party (not connected to the tenant), a chance event or by the landlord himself.

MAINTENANCE AND REPAIR

The property must be maintained and the tenant (unlike his UK counterpart) is responsible for most routine maintenance and repairs (Article 7d). Replacing an electric socket or a tap would fall into this category. Routine servicing of the central heating boiler would also be included here and the landlord can ask to see the relevant maintenance contract.

ACCESS TO THE PROPERTY

Where major works need to be carried out by the landlord the tenant must allow access to the property (Article 7e). If the work lasts more than 40 days, however, he can ask for a reduction in the rent for the inconvenience (article 1724 of the Civil Code). If the property becomes unusable the tenant can terminate the contract.

ALTERATIONS TO THE PROPERTY

Major alterations to the property are not allowed (Article 7f) without written permission from the landlord. Surprisingly, however, a tenant can change the carpet or repaint the walls! Where major alterations have been carried out without permission the landlord can insist on everything being returned to its original condition, at the tenant's expense, before the keys are handed back.

INSURANCE

In the UK it is the landlord's responsibility to insure the property, whether it is furnished or not. In France it is the tenant who must insure an unfurnished property (the landlord assuming the responsibility if the property is furnished). At the very least the tenant must insure against damage caused by fire, water and explosion (Article 7g). The landlord has a right to check the insurance documents every year. Failure to comply with this requirement can result in the contract being terminated.

CHARGES

The tenant is naturally responsible for his own utility bills but will also be expected to share the maintenance cost of the building where this is applicable. This could include the cost of the caretaker and other staff. However, if a one-off pest control treatment is required for rats (*dératisation*) or insects (*désinsectisation*) the landlord will pay the bill. Where a local tax is levied for rubbish collection (*taxe d'enlèvement des ordures ménagères*) the tenant pays. These charges are usually added to the monthly rent and adjusted annually where necessary. If the tenant leaves with unpaid bills the landlord can pursue payment for up to five years, in the case of unpaid taxes, and for 30 years for other unpaid bills.

17

Furnished and Unfurnished

The 1989 legislation concentrated on unfurnished letting (*location vide*), excluding furnished letting (*location meublée*) from most of its provisions. To a large extent the gap between the two has now been bridged by the *loi de Cohesion Sociale* or *loi Borloo* of 18 January 2005. This Act brought unfurnished and furnished lettings closer together. Some important differences, however, still remain.

The *loi Borloo* tightened the rules where the furnished accommodation is the *principal residence* of the tenant. Where this is the case some important legal requirements apply:

1. A verbal agreement alone is not acceptable. The contract (*bail*) must be in writing and have attached a full list of the furniture provided in the property.

2. The minimum term is one year, renewable automatically (*tacite reconduction*) unless notice is given by either party. For a student let the term can be nine months, with no automatic renewal.

3. Notice (*congé*) to end the tenancy must be given in writing by the landlord three months in advance and can only take effect at the end of the tenancy term. The notice period (*délai de préavis*) starts when the tenant has signed his receipt of the written notice. The tenant can end the tenancy at any time

(even before the end of the term) by giving one month's notice in writing.

4. While the tenant is not required to renew the contract the landlord can only fail to do so for one of three reasons – because he wishes to sell the property, live in it himself (the landlord or his immediate family) or because the tenant has been in breach of his contract (e.g. non-payment of rent, damage to property etc.).

5. The rent can be set by agreement between the parties but any increase can only take place on renewal and after three months' notice. The increase must be in line with the annual construction cost index (*Indice du Coût de la Construction* or ICC). For a new tenancy with a new tenant there are no restrictions on the rent that can be agreed.

6. There are no restrictions on the deposit that can be required for a furnished letting.

7. Responsibility for insuring the property rests with the landlord, not the tenant.

It is important to bear in mind that these rules apply only where the accommodation is the tenant's **principal residence**. While there is no definition of 'principal residence' it is accepted that a short-term holiday let (up to 90 days) would not come under this category as the tenant clearly has a *principal residence* elsewhere.

The meaning of 'furnished' can also give rise to confusion as there is, likewise, no definition of this term. It is accepted, however, that the tenant should have everything he needs for day-to-day living without having to bring in additional furniture or equipment of his own. A fridge and cooker in working order, for example, would be expected, along with tables, chairs, beds and other essentials.

The question of whether the property is 'furnished' or not is a matter of no little importance to the landlord. In the event of a legal dispute there is always the risk that a court would reclassify the property as 'unfurnished', placing the tenancy on a very different footing indeed.

The following table sets out the principal similarities and differences between furnished and unfurnished lettings:

Table 17.1   Similarities and differences between furnished and unfurnished lettings

	Furnished	Unfurnished
Contract	Must be in writing if tenant's main home.	Must be in writing, whatever the circumstances.
Term	1 year minimum, renewable.	3 years minimum, renewable. 12 months possible if landlord is due to retire or his child will need the property to pursue his studies.
Landlord notice	3 months before end of contract.	6 months before end of contract.
Tenant notice	1 month at any time.	3 months at any time, reduced to 1 month if in poor health, over 60 or in receipt of income support (RMI or *revenu minimum d'insertion*). Also if starting a new job or being transferred.

Landlord's right to end contract	Only if the property is needed for himself or his family, if he plans to sell it or if the tenant is in breach of contract.	Only if the property is needed for himself or his family, if he plans to sell it or if the tenant is in breach of contract.
Deposit	No limit set. Can't be increased on renewal.	1 month maximum. Can't be increased on renewal.
Future increases in rent	There must be an indexation clause in the lease and increases must be in line with the construction cost index.	There must be an indexation clause in the lease and increases must be in line with the construction cost index.
Tenant's right of pre-emption	No.	Yes. It must be exercised within 2 months of receiving landlord's notice of his intention to sell.
Insurance	Landlord's responsibility.	Tenant must obtain insurance to cover fire, flood and explosion, renew the insurance annually and provide landlord with confirmation from insurer.
Inventory required	Yes.	Yes.

18

Support for Tenants and Landlords

A striking feature of the French system is the high level of financial support for tenants provided through various government sponsored bodies. All tenants or prospective tenants have a right to seek assistance. There are clear benefits for the landlord in these arrangements.

RENT SUBSIDY

For the tenant already in occupation there is the possibility of having part of the rent paid for him by *la Caisse d'Allocations Familiales* (CAF). Not everyone will qualify, however. To see whether he meets the criteria the applicant begins by completing an online questionnaire (anonymous at this stage) on the CAF website (see *Help for tenants* in Appendix C). The *simulation logement* is a simple question and answer programme starting with the postcode of the tenant's property and moving on to ask about the type of accommodation, whether it is furnished or not, whether the tenant lives alone or shares the property, the monthly rent, date of birth of tenant and partner, number of children under 21, whether the tenant is working (employed or self-employed, full or part time), whether he is unable to work through long-term illness, his salary level, other sources of income (such as pension or invalidity benefit) and expenses apart from rent. Any student with a tenancy agreement in his name can apply. At the end of the process the tenant is told if he is entitled to claim and how much he would be allowed on a monthly basis. He then downloads an application form and returns it with the required documentary evidence (*pièces justificatives*).

RENTAL GUARANTEE

Through an organisation called *Action Logement* (formerly known as *1% logement*) it is possible for many prospective tenants to obtain a guarantee for the landlord that the rent will be paid if the tenant defaults. This is known as **Garantie LOCA-PASS**. It is available for employees in the private sector (non-agricultural) regardless of age, salary, work or type of rented accommodation. It also covers young people under 30 on work experience or looking for work, students and retired workers from the private sector (non-agricultural) who have been retired for less than five years.

The request for this guarantee cannot be made *after* the tenancy agreement is signed. The guarantee itself must be attached to the tenancy agreement.

While there is no charge for the guarantee the tenant does enter into a legally binding agreement. If the guarantee has to be invoked by the landlord the tenant undertakes to repay the sum involved, interest free, to *Action Logement* (see *Help for tenants* in Appendix C) over a three-year period.

From a landlord's perspective the *Garantie LOCA-PASS* is as good as it gets. This is the gold standard of guarantees, a *caution solidaire* – a guarantee binding on all parties.

LOAN OF DEPOSIT

Through the same organisation (*Action Logement*) it is possible to provide the tenant with the deposit required by the landlord, up to a limit of €2,300, in the form of a loan (*prêt*). This is known as *Avance LOCA-PASS*.

The loan is interest free and is repaid over three years. The minimum monthly payment is €15 and repayments start three months after the loan is made. Where a tenant leaves the property before the end of the three-year period he must repay the loan in full within three months of his departure. The deposit can be paid directly to the landlord if the tenant prefers. Where the tenant is provided with short-term accommodation (e.g. for seasonal work) he can repay the loan in one go when he leaves, provided the tenancy is for six months or less. In the case of hostel or social housing accommodation a commitment to pay the deposit, if required, can take the place of an immediate loan.

The loans are only available where the accommodation is to be the tenant's principal residence and there can be only one loan per property. When it is repaid the tenant will qualify for another loan for another property. It is possible to have both the *Avance LOCA-PASS* and the *Garantie LOCA-PASS* for the same property.

Action Logement undertakes to process all fully completed applications within eight days of receipt. If the applicant hasn't had a decision in that time the loan is automatically agreed. If he is rejected he can appeal to the *Conseil d'Administration du Comité Interprofessionnel du Logement* (CIL) or the local Chamber of Commerce – *Bureau de la Chambre de Commerce et d'Industrie* (CCI). If he is refused again he can take his appeal to the *Conseil d'Administration de l'UESL (Fédération d'Action Logement)*. See Appendix C under *Help for tenants*.

INSURANCE FOR TENANTS

Landlords and agents naturally favour prospective tenants who qualify for the *Avance LOCA-PASS*, the *Garantie LOCA-PASS* or both. Tenants who don't can be at a serious disadvantage. This is particularly the case when they can't meet the usual requirement of having an income three or four times the monthly rent.

To encourage landlords to accept such tenants there is an insurance scheme, operated by *GRL Gestion* (see Appendix C) which covers the landlord against the important risks associated with letting his property – non-payment of rent and damage to the property. The tenant is provided with a 'passport' of guarantee or **PASS-GRL** – effectively an insurance policy to cover such risks (*Garantie des Risques Locatifs*) – to present to the landlord or agent. The tenant can check online to see if he qualifies to make an application.

The scheme is primarily intended to cover situations where the rent demanded will be 33%–50% of the tenant's income. The rent will be guaranteed up to €2,300 per month for the duration of the contract. It dispenses with the need for a deposit, guaranteeing to pay up to €7,700 for damage caused by the tenant. Where litigation is required the landlord's legal fees will be met. The landlord or agent is provided with instructions on how to make a claim.

While the scheme is intended to help people looking for accommodation it can also be available in some circumstances where the tenant is already in occupation. In this case the tenant must be up to date with his rent and must not have missed more than two consecutive months (in whole or part) in the previous six months. The contract must have been in place for at least six months before the application for a *PASS-GRL*.

As this is an insurance scheme it carries an insurance premium. It is not, however, paid by the tenant. An agent will be charged 1.8% inc VAT (*TVA*) of the annual rent while the private landlord will pay 2.5% (including VAT). These premiums are paid quarterly. The cost is a deductible allowance against the *Taxe Foncièrè* (see Chapter 24). A list of agents participating in the scheme is available on the *GRL Gestion* website.

RELOCATION COSTS

There can be circumstances when finding somewhere else to live is a matter of necessity rather than choice. Starting a new job is one such case. Another is when an employer relocates to a new address. In both of these cases financial assistance may be available.

The scheme, called **AIDE MOBILI-PASS**, is available through *Action Logement* for tenants and owner-occupiers alike who work in the private sector (not agricultural). The nature of the work contract is irrelevant although the company must have ten employees or more for an employee to qualify. Large public sector companies which contribute to *Action Logement* will also qualify. The new address must be at least 70 km from the old and the application for assistance must be made within six months of the event that triggers it (new job or employer relocation). It is available to the same applicant only once every two years.

Expenses covered are agent's fees, legal fees, mortgage-related costs and, if the move involves maintaining two homes, the first six months' rent in the new property. There is a maximum grant of €1,600 if the application is made independently of the employer. Where there is a written agreement with the employer the limit is €3,200. Bills and invoices are required. Where an application is rejected an appeal can be made to the *Conseil d'Administration du Comité Interprofessionnel du Logement* (CIL) or the local Chamber of Commerce – *Bureau de la Chambre de Commerce et d'Industrie* (CCI). If this fails a further appeal can be made to the *Conseil d'Administration de l'UESL* (*Fédération d'Action Logement*). See *Help for tenants* in Appendix C.

UNFORESEEN EVENTS

It is not possible to plan for everything and some unexpected events can have dire financial consequences – divorce, separation, redundancy, illness, death of a breadwinner, unmanageable debt. Advice and practical help under these circumstances is provided by the **CIL-PASS assistance**, available through *CIL-CCI* (*comité interprofessionnel du logement*).

Available to employees in companies with ten or more on the staff, the scheme provides tailored advice with introductions to other agencies for practical help. This can include a temporary loan to make rent or mortgage payments, repayment of debt or help in finding alternative accommodation. There is no charge for this service.

Given the huge importance of the rental sector in France it is not surprising that some state assistance is aimed directly at the **landlord**. It comes, however, with strings attached.

AGENCE NATIONALE DE L'HABITAT

A landlord can qualify for a property tax reduction and a grant to carry out works in the property if he is prepared to register with the *Agence nationale de l'habitat* (ANAH). Non-resident landlords can also join the scheme (see *State help for landlords* in Appendix C).

The property in question must be unfurnished and either available to let or already let as a principal residence. If already let the registration would take effect on the contract renewal date. It will not be accepted if it is let to a member of the landlord's family. It must constitute a *logement décent* as set out in the 6 July 1989 Act (see Chapter 15) and the tenancy agreement must comply with the same law.

The landlord must accept certain conditions – a cap on the rent he can charge and a six-year agreement with the agency (nine years if he requires a grant to carry out work). ANAH issues a scale of rents which will always be lower than local market rents. In return the landlord will get a reduction of 30% on his *Taxe Foncière* (see Chapter 24) and access to a grant to improve the property.

INSURANCE FOR LANDLORDS

Landlords can help themselves by taking out insurance to cover the risk of unpaid rent and other financial loss resulting from letting his property. This type of insurance (*Assurance Loyers Impayés* or *Garantie Locative*) is provided by insurance companies and the premium (*prime d'assurance*) can be between 2% and 4% of the annual rent. It is available for furnished and unfurnished lettings (but not holiday lets).

Note, however, that a landlord cannot have both a third-party guarantee (*caution solidaire*) and this kind of insurance. If he opts for the insurance he can't ask the tenant for a guarantee.

There are typically three areas covered by this form of insurance:

Unpaid rent

After four months of unpaid rent the landlord will receive three months' rent which, together with the tenant's deposit, brings the rent up to date. Payments will continue to be made for a maximum of 24 months. There is normally a cap on the monthly payments (e.g. €3,000).

Damage to property

At the end of the tenancy the deposit will normally cover the cost of any damage (*dégradation*) caused by the tenant. If the deposit is not sufficient for this, however, the insurance will provide the difference and also compensate the landlord for loss of rent while work is being carried out. A limit will be set for the cost of repairs (e.g. €8,000) and the compensation for lost rent (e.g. two months' rent at a maximum of €3,000 pm).

Legal costs

In the event of legal action to recover rent or evict a tenant the insurance company will pay the bill, up to an agreed maximum (e.g. €4,000).

Insurance companies take considerable care when taking on this risk and may require sight of all important documentation relating to the tenancy. In particular they will expect to see an up-to-date and legal tenancy agreement (*contrat de bail*), a thorough *état des lieux* (see Chapter 15) and a full set of tenant references (showing an income at least 3 × the monthly rent). He will also be expected to have obtained the maximum deposit allowed.

Cover can be obtained directly from insurance companies (see *Rental insurance for landlords* in Appendix C) or through an insurance broker (*courtier en assurances*). It is sometimes available through letting agents as part of their service to landlords (see Chapter 20).

The premiums are deductible against *Taxe Foncière* (see Chapter 24).

19

The Tenancy Agreement

A written tenancy agreement (*contrat de bail*) is required whether the property is furnished or not. If it is drawn up by a *notaire* or an agent the fee for this must be shared between landlord and tenant. If the landlord produces his own contract he cannot charge the tenant. Two copies of the contract are required, one for the landlord and one for the tenant. If there is a guarantor he must also be provided with a copy.

As there are still some differences between furnished and unfurnished letting the contracts required for each are not identical.

UNFURNISHED CONTRACT

The Act of 6 July 1989 leaves nothing to chance when it comes to unfurnished lettings. Article 3 of the Act sets out precisely what the contract must contain, what is optional and what is expressly forbidden.

The parties

As might be expected the parties to the contract must be named. In the case of the landlord, however, his address must also be provided. If the landlord is a company the company's head office (*siège social*) must be listed. Where an agent is used his name and address must also feature in the contract.

Start date and term

The date the tenancy starts must be entered. This can differ from the date the contract is signed or the date the tenant takes up residence. The term of the tenancy must be at least three years from the start date. If the landlord is a company the minimum term is six years.

Description of property and intended use

The type of property (apartment, house) and the number of rooms must be indicated, together with details of contents and equipment provided for the tenant's use and which the tenant will be expected to maintain – carpets, blinds, curtains, mirrors, central heating, water heater, radiators, toilet, shower, bath etc. If there is a garage, cellar (*cave*) or garden these must also be included.

The contract will state if the property is for residential use only or for residential and business use (*à usage mixte*). If it is for residential use only it will not be possible to run a business without written consent from the landlord.

Rent

The rent (excluding charges) must be stated as well as the date payment is due. It must also be made clear whether payment is to be made monthly or quarterly, in advance (*à échoir*) or in arrears (*à terme échu*).

Rent review (optional)

If the rent is to be reviewed annually this must be stated in the contract. Otherwise, no review is possible. Where a rent review (*révision du loyer*) is planned the date of the first review should be indicated and a statement made to the effect that the review will be based on the Cost of Construction Index (*Indice du Coût de la Construction*) published by the *Institut national de la statistique et des études économiques* (INSEE).

Deposit (optional)

If a deposit (*dépôt de garantie*) is required the amount must be stated in the contract along with details of how and when it is to be returned. It cannot exceed one month's rent, excluding charges. No deposit can be demanded where the rent is payable quarterly in advance or where there is no reference to a deposit in the contract.

Grounds for termination (optional)

The landlord can choose to insert a clause setting out grounds for bringing the tenancy agreement to an end (*clause résolutoire*). The law, however, allows only three such grounds – non-payment of rent, non-payment of deposit (where a deposit is specified in the contract) and failure to insure the property.

Third party guarantee (optional)

Where a landlord is not happy with the financial background of his prospective tenant he can require a guarantee (*caution*) from a third party (e.g. a parent). Where this is the case there must be a clause to that effect in the contract.

Planned work (optional)

If the property is not quite ready the tenant may offer to carry out some improvements when he moves in. Where both parties agree the details of this arrangement (the work, the cost and who will pay) must be set out in the contract.

Joint liability (optional)

Where a property is let to sharers the landlord may want to ensure that the rent will be paid in full, even if one of his tenants fails to pay his share. To this end he can insert a *clause solidaire* in the contract making all the tenants jointly responsible for the rent. If one fails to pay the others must make up the difference.

Invalid clauses

Not content with listing the compulsory and optional clauses in the contract the 1989 Act (article 4) expressly rules out a whole list of clauses, declaring them invalid and unenforceable, if they were to be included. These are:

1. Any requirement for payment by direct debit from the tenant's bank account (*prélèvement automatique*) or in the form of a deduction by his employer from his salary.

2. A clause stating grounds for termination (*résiliation*) other than non-payment of rent, non payment of the deposit or failure to insure the property.

3. A clause forbidding the keeping of non-dangerous pets.

4. Any restriction on the use of the property for political, union or religious activities.

5. A clause imposing fines (*amendes*) for a breach of contract.

6. A requirement that the tenant insure the property with an insurance company chosen by the landlord.

7. A clause allowing the landlord to visit the property on holidays or for more than two hours per visit.

Annexes to contract

At the time the contract is signed the tenant must have a copy of the inventory (*état des lieux*). This must be attached to the contract. If the property to be let is an apartment in a *copropriété* (see Chapter 7) certain extracts from the *copropriété* rules must also be annexed. These deal with the use to which the apartment can be put (residential, mixed use etc.), rules relating to the common parts of the building and the share of the charges applicable to the apartment. In all cases an energy performance certificate (*diagnostic de performance énergétique*) must be attached.

FURNISHED CONTRACT

While most of the clauses in an unfurnished contract will appear in the furnished version there are far fewer obligatory clauses and some significant differences should be noted.

Term (obligatory)

For a furnished letting, as a principal residence, the minimum term is one year (not three). If the tenant is a student this can be reduced to nine months.

Tenant notice (obligatory)

There must be a clause to the effect that the tenant can give one month's notice at any time in the course of the tenancy.

Landlord notice and renewal (obligatory)

For the landlord the notice period is three months and he must wait till the end of the tenancy to gain possession. Reasons for not renewing the contract are the same as for an unfurnished let (i.e. he needs the property for himself or his family, he wishes to sell or the tenant is in default). In the case of a furnished let, however, he can also regain possession if he serves notice (three months) that he will require changes to the contract (e.g. the rent) and if the tenant refuses to accept these changes. In this case the contract ends and need not be renewed. If the tenant is a student on a nine-month contract there is no requirement to renew and no automatic renewal (*tacite reconduction du bail*).

WHERE TO GET A CONTRACT

A contract can be provided by a letting agent or drawn up by a *notaire*. It can also be downloaded for free or for as little as €2 from many websites. A Google search for *contrat de bail* will yield an ample choice. A commonly used provider of contracts is *Tissot* (see Appendix C). Given the critical nature of this document, however, it is essential that it is legally watertight and absolutely up to date. For that reason the only safe source is a *notaire*.

20

Finding Tenants

Most estate agents (*agents immobiliers*) are deeply involved in the long-term lettings market. It is common to find their activities split into sales and letting, with separate departments devoted to each. There are also many agents who deal exclusively in letting and managing property (*gestion immobilière*). Having said that, however, it is perfectly possible to ignore agents altogether and do everything yourself.

THE LETTING AGENT

Letting agents, like sales agents, are regulated by the *Loi Hoguet* of January 1970 (see Chapter 4) and must have a licence or *carte professionnelle* to practice. While the sales agent needs a carte 'T' (*transactions sur immeubles et fonds de commerce*), the letting agent (*gestionnaire immobilier* or *administrateur de biens*) must have a *carte* 'G' (*gestion immobilière*), obtained from the local *Préfecture* and renewed annually. This guarantees that the agent is properly qualified to operate in the lettings market, has adequate financial guarantees to safeguard any deposits, has an appropriate level of indemnity insurance and has not been disqualified from acting as a letting agent. A letting agent will also be expected to belong to one of the professional bodies (see Chapter 4) such as *Fédération Nationale de l'Immobilier* (FNAIM) or *Professionnels Immobiliers* (SNPI). Details of the *carte professionnelle*, membership of professional body and level of financial guarantee must feature on the agent's letterheads and literature.

Services offered

Most letting agents offer a full management service and will take responsibility for all aspects of letting and management of the property. They will value the property for rental purposes, find tenants, run checks, take up references, arrange viewings, draw up contracts, collect deposits and rent, draw up an inventory (*état des lieux*), check tenants in and out, carry out regular inspections of the property, organise repairs when necessary, renew contracts and review the rent annually.

The landlord can expect to receive monthly payments of the rent (less the agent's fees and expenses) by cheque or bank transfer (*virement*). Regular statements of expenses and an end-of-year balance should always be provided.

Some agents include insurance against unpaid rent (*assurance loyers impayés* or *garantie locative*) as part of their management package or as an optional extra. In either case the cover is considerably cheaper than it would be if bought independently by the landlord (see Chapter 18).

Cost

Agents' fees (*honoraires*) for a full management service can vary considerably, depending on local competition and whether rental insurance is included – between 5.5% and 8.5% (including *TVA*) of the annual rent. Where the agent is commissioned just to find a tenant and draw up the contract the standard fee is two months' rent, split between landlord and tenant.

Agency agreement

The agent must be formally authorised to act for the landlord through a *mandat de gestion locative* or *mandat d'administration de biens* (letting and management agreement).

The agreement details the name and address of the landlord (referred to as the 'principal' or *mandant*) and the agent (*mandataire*), along with the address and description of the property to be let, a full list of the services the agent undertakes to perform and the fees payable by the landlord. It will also state how rent will be paid to the landlord and how often he will be provided with a statement of account.

Details of the agent's indemnity insurance, financial guarantees, membership of professional bodies and licence held must all feature in the document.

If the agreement is to constitute a sole agency (*mandat, avec exclusivité*) to find a tenant this must be clearly stated. Such a clause prevents the landlord from using another agent or finding a tenant himself. Alternatively, it can be limited in time (e.g. three months, renewable) and specifically *not* a sole agency (*sans exclusivité*).

An agreement to let *and* manage the property will normally be on a sole agency basis for one year (from the date the agreement is signed), renewable automatically (*tacite reconduction*) unless cancelled by either party. The *mandat* will stipulate the notice period required to end the agreement – usually three months before the renewal date. The notice must be in writing and sent registered post (*letter recommandé avec avis de réception*).

An unfortunate complication of this standard clause is that the task of both finding the tenant and managing the property are lumped together. In other words, the *mandant* is committed for one year even if the agent fails to find a tenant at all during that time!

Before the *mandat* is signed the agent will require proof of the landlord's identity, such as passport or identity card (*carte d'identité*), proof of ownership of the property (property tax bill, *notaire*'s *attestation* of purchase) and bank account details.

Tips

If using an agent, don't accept the standard sole agency agreement. Negotiate more flexible terms on the all-important timescale envisaged for signing up your first tenant. If a tenant is not found within an agreed time you should be free to go elsewhere.

DO-IT-YOURSELF

While it is clearly tempting to let an agent do all the work, the internet has made it very easy to avoid agents altogether and to do it yourself – provided, of course, you are confident in your language skills and have the time to deal with the enquiries.

Websites

There are several sites which will take advertisements from private individuals (*particuliers*) as well as from agents. Some cater only for private advertisements. Some have sister publications and will also place the advert in a local or regional paper. Most sites charge for the service but some are free.

The procedure for placing an advertisement is broadly the same on all sites. If there is a charge for the service the site will display the prices (*tarifs*) applicable for property adverts and invite you to place one (*passer une annonce*). Contact details – address, email address and telephone – will be required. Readers will be invited to respond by phone or by email through the site.

For the most popular sites see *Advertising for landlords* in Appendix C.

The advertisement

There is normally little space restriction on a website advertisement and consequently the property can be described in full and in detail. The situation is different, however, in the newspaper version. Here space is at a premium.

The essential details in a French property advertisement (to let or sell) are the surface area of the property, the number of rooms (*pièces*) apart from the kitchen and bathroom and the rent. In newspaper advertisements there is often little reference to anything else. To economise still further abbreviations are commonly used, such as *asc* (*ascenseur* or 'lift') and codes such as T1, T2 etc. (or F1, F2) to denote a property with one or two rooms. A one-bedroom apartment is thus T2 (two rooms). A two-bedroom apartment with a lift would be T3, asc.

It is important to be familiar with the vocabulary and jargon used in property advertisements. For the most common phrases and expressions, see Appendix B.

If you decide to go down the DIY route leave nothing to chance. Use a *notaire* to draw up the *contrat de bail* (Chapter 10). Take all possible references, inspect original documents and keep copies

(Chapter 15). Only accept a tenant with an income at least 3 x the monthly rent (Chapter 15). Look for tenants with the *Avance LOCA-PASS*, the *Garantie LOCA-PASS* or both (Chapter 18). Always take a deposit (Chapter 15). Do a thorough *état des lieux* (Chapter 15). Take out rental insurance (Chapter 18).

THE STUDENT MARKET

If you decide to buy in a university town (see Chapter 2) and are happy to let to students, you will be kept busy!

There are three sources of accommodation for students in France – university halls of residence, hostels and the private sector.

In the case of halls of residence there is limited availability and priority is given to students on grants (*étudiants boursiers*). Students apply through the *Centres Régionaux des Œuvres Universitaires et Scolaires* or CROUS (each university town has an office) and typically try to secure accommodation between January and April for the term commencing the following September. Single rooms and studios are offered at very competitive rates.

Hostel accommodation (*foyers d'étudiants*) is available for students between 16 and 25. These are often run by religious organisations and are sometimes single-sex only. As a result they are not universally popular. Applications are made through the *Union nationale des maisons d'étudiants* (UNME).

Private accommodation, although the most expensive of the options available, is in great demand. Peak time for the private landlord is June when the *Baccalauréat* (*bac*) exams begin. Timing is of the essence here. Advertisements by private landlords or their agents appear in early June. The target publication for students is *ParuVendu* which appears in print form on a Thursday and on the net at www.paruvendu.fr (see Appendix C). It should also be noted that CROUS (see above) also offers space for private landlords to advertise on their site (see Appendix C).

Finally, it is worth remembering that students are entitled to apply for a rent subsidy through *Caisse d'Allocations Familiales* or CAF (see Chapter 18).

Part Five

TAX

21

Income Tax

Both the UK and the French tax authorities have an interest in any rental income generated in France by a UK resident. The good news, however, is that nobody pays twice. The Double Tax Treaty with France means that tax paid in France by a UK resident can be offset against his UK tax liability. If the UK tax bill is higher the difference will have to be paid to the UK Revenue. There is no rebate, however, if the UK tax bill is lower!

It follows that tax returns will have to be filed in both countries. In France the tax year and the calendar year coincide, with the tax becoming due in the year after it has been incurred. There are special arrangements for non-residents with regards to filing deadlines and the address to which tax returns should be sent (see below).

FRENCH TAX CALCULATION

There is a distinction, for tax purposes, between furnished and unfurnished letting in France.

Unfurnished

For unfurnished lettings there are two tax regimes available – a simplified system where the rental income is below €15,000 for the year and a more complicated system for income in excess of that figure.

The simplified system, known as *micro-foncier*, requires only that the gross rental income be recorded in the tax return. A flat 30% will be deducted for expenses (no invoices, receipts, bills or itemised costs required) from this figure and the remaining 70% will be taxed at 20%. Note that if the property has been bought through a company structure (SCI) the *micro-foncier* regime is not available.

The second system (*régime réel*) applies if the rent exceeds €15,000 but this is also available as an option to anyone who might benefit from it (it should be noted that if this option is chosen it cannot be revoked for three years). In this case, in addition to declaring the gross rental income, all expenses are itemised – maintenance costs, interest on a French mortgage (used to buy the property), property taxes, insurance, management costs (all relevant paperwork, receipts etc. must be available), professional fees. These costs will be deducted from the gross rent and the balance taxed at 20%. Losses incurred can be carried forward for up to ten years against future rental income. This regime will be of special interest to anyone who has taken out a French mortgage to buy the property as the interest on the mortgage can be offset against the rental income.

Furnished

There is a similar arrangement for furnished lettings, but with different figures. In this case the simplified regime (*micro-bic*) applies to rental income under €32,000. The gross income is declared and a flat 50% deducted for expenses. The balance is then taxed at 20%. For registered *gîtes ruraux, chambres d'hôtes* and *meublés de tourisme* (such as most leaseback properties) the maximum rent allowable is €80,000 with 71% deducted before tax is levied. Note that if the property has been bought through a company (SCI) and is then let *furnished* the tax applicable will be corporation tax, not income tax.

For rental income above these levels the *régime réel* applies and expenses have to be itemised (receipts, invoices etc. must be available if required). These costs are deducted from the gross income and the balance taxed at 20%. As with unfurnished lettings this regime can be chosen by anyone, whatever his income, if it would be beneficial. Losses incurred can be carried forward for up to ten years against future rental income. This regime will be of special interest to anyone who has taken out a French mortgage to buy the property as the interest on the mortgage can be offset against the rental income.

A further complication for the landlord of furnished property is the distinction made between *professional* and *non-professional* letting. For a landlord to be classed as professional (*loueur en meublé professionnel*) his rental income must exceed €23,000. This, in turn, must be more than 50% of his total annual income. If both these criteria are met he can register with the *registre du commerce et des sociétés* so that he can be classified as 'professional'. You might well ask why bother? The answer is that for the French resident there are several tax advantages in the 'professional landlord' classification – losses on rental income can be offset against *all* income (not just rental income); valued added tax (*TVA*) paid can be reclaimed; capital gains tax falls to zero after just five years if income for the year the property was sold has not exceeded €90,000 (inclusive of *TVA*). For the non-resident landlord. however, (subject as he is to the tax regime of his country of residence) there may be little of interest in the 'professional landlord' status. It should also be noted that the professional landlord will normally be expected to pay an additional social welfare levy of 15.5% on the rental income, though he will be exempted from the occupancy tax (*taxe d'habitation*).

FRENCH BUDGET 2013 AND INCOME TAX

The new government of François Hollande ruffled a good many feathers in the UK with his budget proposals regarding second homes in France owned by non-residents. The proposal, in a nutshell, is to add the **social charge of 15.5%** to the tax on any income or capital gain from such properties. At the moment only French residents are subject to the charge. This would mean that rental income for non-residents would be subject to a levy of 35.5% (20% tax + 15.5% social charge). This compares with UK income tax rates of 20% for a basic rate taxpayer or 40% at the higher rate. The plan is to make this change retrospective to 1 January 2012.

The first point to note about this proposal, as it stands, is that it refers to *unfurnished* properties only. Holiday lets (which are always furnished) and long-term furnished lets would not be affected. This loophole could, of course, be closed in the future.

Secondly, there will undoubtedly be a legal challenge to this measure. If it stands, other EU citizens, not resident in France, will be obliged to pay for French social services from which they cannot benefit. A clear case of discrimination.

If the measure goes ahead and survives a legal challenge the following would be the outcome for the UK resident:

The basic rate taxpayer would face an additional cost of 15.5% (35.5% instead of 20%). For the higher rate taxpayer the outcome would depend on the attitude of the UK Revenue to the social charge. If they treat it as a tax then the full 35.5% would be allowable against UK tax and only 4.5% additional tax would be due to the Revenue. If, however, they don't accept the social charge as a tax, only 20% would be allowable and an additional 20% would therefore be payable to the UK Revenue, bumping up the total charge for the higher rate tax payer to 55.5%.

FORMS AND FILING DEADLINES

A tax return must be submitted annually for rental income incurred in the previous tax year. For non-residents returns are made to:

Centre des Impôts des Non-Résidents (CINR)
TSA 10010
10 rue du Centre
93465 Noisy-le-Grand Cedex
France

The relevant forms are 2042, 2042C and 2044 which can be obtained by post from the *Centre des Impôts des Non-Résidents* or downloaded from www.impots.gouv.fr.

For rental income from unfurnished letting, where the *micro-foncier* regime applies (i.e. the income is less than €15,000), form 2042 needs to be completed. Apart from personal details of name, date of birth and country of residence, the rental income is simply declared gross (*brut*) in box BE.

If the *régime réel* applies (i.e. the income is more than €15,000 or the tax payer chooses this regime) forms 2042 and 2044 must be completed. In 2044 declare the gross income and list all expenses. Transfer the resulting profit or loss figure to form 2042, section 4.

For furnished lettings 2042 and 2042C need to be completed. 2042 simply requires name, date of birth, country of residence and a signature. In form 2042C declare the gross income in section 5, box NO or, if the property is jointly owned, boxes NO and OO.

The filing deadline for residents of Europe, North America and Africa is 30 June. For residents of Central and South America, it is 15 July.

UK TAX CALCULATION

A tax return must also be submitted in the UK where there is rental income from property owned abroad, although the Double Tax Treaty with France ensures that no one is taxed twice.

The tax calculation is less complicated but, in many cases, less advantageous than the French version. There is no simplified system corresponding to the *micro-foncier* or *micro-bic*, no distinction between furnished and unfurnished, no 'professional' and 'non-professional' status. There is consequently no notional figure for expenses that can be deducted automatically from the gross income. Whatever the income, all allowable expenses actually incurred must be totted up and deducted from the gross figure. The result is a profit or loss for that tax year. Profits are taxed but losses cannot be offset against other UK income, even UK property income. They are carried forward to the next tax year.

Allowable expenses include repairs, maintenance, management costs, advertising, travel costs (exclusively for the business), agent's fees, cleaner's fees, utility bills and local property taxes if paid by the owner, insurance premiums and interest on a UK mortgage to buy the property. There is also an energy savings allowance of up to £1,500 per property for loft, wall and floor insulation, draught-proofing and insulating hot water systems. For furnished properties a 10% wear and tear allowance can be claimed. Also allowed is any tax on the income already paid in France. Naturally, records must be kept of all income and expenses.

FORMS AND FILING DEADLINES

A general Self-Assessment tax form must be completed even if this has not been required before. This should be obtained from the taxpayer's regional tax office. In addition to this the Foreign Pages supplementary form SA 106 must be completed for the foreign property income. This can be downloaded from the Revenue's website at www.hmrc.gov.uk.

Most UK resident taxpayers with income generated abroad will pay tax on that income, whether it is brought back to the UK or not. However, UK residents who are not domiciled or ordinarily resident in the UK can choose to be taxed on a remittance basis, that is only on the income actually brought into the country. For everyone else, however, foreign income is taxed as it arises. This is known as the 'arising basis'. Where it is not possible to remit income because, for example, of exchange controls, a claim can be made not to have this income taxed when it would otherwise be taxed on the arising basis. Page F1 of form SA106 allows the taxpayer to choose between these options.

The remaining pages to complete are F4 and F5. Here the income and expenses are detailed. If there is more than one property the income from all together is declared. Expenses are likewise taken together. For furnished property the 10% reduction for wear and tear is claimed here as is the landlord's energy saving allowance, if applicable (see above). Where foreign tax has already been paid this can now be declared and deducted (alternatively, a claim for foreign tax credit relief can be made on page F1). Where the owner also makes personal use of the property (most commonly in the case of holiday lets) expenses cannot be claimed for such private use. The non-business element of the expenses must be detailed on page F5.

The result is a profit or loss for that tax year. Profits are taxed at the taxpayer's marginal rate but losses cannot be offset against other UK income, even UK property income. They are carried forward to the next tax year.

Unfortunately, the tax year in the UK is from 6 April to 5 April and so does not correspond to the calendar year as it does in France. Careful record keeping is essential, with particular attention paid to dates, so as to allocate the correct French income to the UK tax year. A further complication is that euros have to be converted to sterling at the exchange rate applicable *at the time the income was received*.

The deadline for filing is 31 October (for paper-based returns) and 31 January (for online returns) in the year following the tax year in question. The forms should be returned to the taxpayer's own tax office.

INCOME TAX INCENTIVES

The French government has always considered the rental market to be of prime importance and has actively encouraged investment in this area through a succession of tax incentive schemes. The latest such scheme is the *Loi Duflot*, which replaced the *Loi Scellier* when it expired at the end of 2012.

Who benefits?

The first thing to bear in mind about this law (and all earlier schemes of this kind) is that it applies only to those investors who are resident in France for tax purposes (*fiscalement domiciliées en France*) and declare *all* their income to the French tax authorities. The UK resident, therefore, who declares only his rental income in France, cannot benefit.

The *Loi Duflot* incentive

To the UK observer the prize offered by the *Loi Duflot* seems extraordinary. The buy-to-let investor can recover 17-20% of the purchase price of a property through annual reductions in his income tax over 9-12 years.

Example	
Property price	200,000
17% of price	34,000
34,000 ÷ 9	3,777
Annual tax reduction for 9 years	3,777

In this case, If the income tax liability in a given year is, say, €20,000, the tax to be paid after the *Loi Duflot* reduction would be €16,223 (20,000 – 3,777). If the total tax liability in a given tax year is less than the *Duflot* refund the 'credit' can be carried forward for six years.

The scheme rules

To qualify under the *scheme* the property purchased must be new (or never lived in), must not cost more than €300,000, must be let at 20% below the market rent and must be located in one of the areas designated for the scheme (where the need for accommodation is most pressing).

Risks

An investment should never be made for tax reasons alone. So attractive are schemes like this that developers and estate agents market them vigorously and, it must be said, not always scrupulously. The risks for the investor are considerable:

- A tenant must be found within 12 months of the purchase. Otherwise the investor fails to qualify under the scheme.

- If there is a gap of more than 12 months between tenancies he loses the tax benefit.

- The same applies if he sells the property within nine years of purchase.

The real danger, therefore, is that the purchase will be made in an area already oversupplied with properties to let, resulting in an empty property, no rental income and no tax benefits – the ultimate nightmare.

22

Capital Gains Tax

Any capital gain on the resale of a property that is not one's main residence is subject to Capital Gains Tax (*impôt sur les plus-values*) in France as it is in the UK. As with income tax, however, the Double Tax Treaty ensures that the tax is not paid twice by the UK resident.

ALLOWANCES

As in the UK certain allowances and expenses can be deducted from the gross gain to arrive at the taxable gain. In France these are:

- For each year after the first five years the property is owned a 2% reduction on the gain can be made until year 15. From years 16 to 25 a 4% abatement applies. From years 26 to 30 the abatement is 8%. After 30 years of ownership no tax is payable and there is no requirement to make a declaration.

- In addition, there is a flat allowance of €1,000.

- Also allowed are costs associated with the purchase and sale of the property. Typically these are the fees paid to the *notaire* and agent. A flat 7.5% of the purchase price can be used in lieu of actual costs.

■ The cost of any capital improvements made to the property is allowable. These must, however, be carried out by professional firms and cannot include routine repairs and maintenance. Any work carried out by the owner himself is excluded. Invoices and receipts are required. If the property has been owned for more than five years a flat 15% of the purchase price can be used in lieu of receipts.

For the non-resident living in another EU country the resulting gain is taxed at 19%. For non EU residents the tax is 33.33%.

FRENCH AND UK CALCULATION

Take the following example of a property bought for €150,000 and sold nine years later for €220,000, realising a profit of €70,000. Calculation for French CGT (*impôt sur les plus-values*) is as follows:

Purchase price	150,000
Transactional costs (*notaire* etc.) at 7.5%	11,250 (150,000 × 7.5%)
Capital improvements @ 15%	22,500 (150,000 × 15%)
Adjusted purchase price	183,750 (150,000 + 11,250 + 22,500)
Adjusted gain	36,250 (220,000 − 183,750)
Flat allowance	1,000
Adjusted gain	35,250 (36,250 − 1000)
8% allowance for years held after first 5 years (4 × 2)	2,820 (35,250 × 8%)
Taxable gain	32,430 (35,250 − 2,820)
Tax @ 19%	6,161

The UK tax regime for capital gains is not as generous. There is no reduction for the number of years the property is held and the tax liability never disappears altogether. Transactional costs and capital improvements costs are allowable but actual receipts are required. The principal concession to the taxpayer is the annual CGT allowance (£10,600 for 2012/13).

The resulting gain will be taxed at 28% (the lower rate of 18% is unlikely to apply as the gain is added to the taxpayer's other income and would, in most cases, take him into the higher rate tax band).

In the above example the calculation for UK tax purposes would be as follows:

Purchase price	150,000
Transactional costs	11,250
Capital improvements	22,500
Adjusted purchase price	183,750 (150,000 + 11,250 + 22,500)
Adjusted gain	36,250 (220,000 − 183,750)
CGT allowance	10,600
Taxable gain	25,650 (36,250 − 10,600)
Tax @ 28%	7,182

In this scenario the British resident would have to pay additional tax of €1,021 (7,182 − 6,161) to the UK Revenue.

EXEMPTIONS

In common with the UK there is no tax to pay on the sale of one's principal residence. In France, however, there are four further circumstances in which no tax at all is payable, whatever the gain. These exemptions also apply to non-residents. They are:

1. Where the vendor is in receipt of a state pension (*pension de vieillesse*) and has not been liable for wealth tax (see below) in the year but one before the sale.

2. Where the property has been owned for more than 30 years.

3. Where the sale price is €20,000 or less.

4. Where a non-resident EU vendor had been tax domiciled in France for a continuous period of two years at any time prior to the sale. This exemption is limited to one property.

Note:

The Finance Bill of 2011 (in effect from 1 February 2012) was amended on 12 October 2011 (largely to help French expats who might find themselves paying CGT on their French home should they decide to sell it after they emigrate).

The amendment provides that if the property was owned for *five years or more* and provided the vendor did not own a principal residence in France for at least *two years*, then the sale would not incur CGT.

What may not have been noticed, however, is that anyone (not only French expats) could arguably benefit from this amendment. A UK resident, for example, who has owned a property in France for five years or more and has not owned a principal residence there for more than two years could also sell his French property and avoid CGT! How long this convenient loophole will remain is another matter, of course. Advice from a *notaire* is essential.

It should be remembered that even if all CGT can be avoided in France the UK resident will be still liable to CGT in the UK. There is no escape!

FRENCH BUDGET 2013 AND CGT

As with Income Tax (see Chapter 21) the 2013 budget in France has implications for CGT.

Good news

Little publicity has been given to the beneficial effects of the budget on CGT. The following changes have been proposed:

1. CGT liability will cease after 22 years of ownership (instead of 30).

2. An abatement of 5% pa (instead of 2%) will apply after just two years (instead of five). In the case of a property held for 15 years under the new scheme the abatement will come to 65%. Under the old system this would be only 20%.

3. If the property is sold within two years any gain will be added to other income for tax purposes. UK residents, however, will have little or no other income in France.

4. Crucially, taper relief will apply after two years to counter the effect of inflation.

5. For *2013 only*, tax relief (*décote*) of **20%** will be available on the gain from investment properties and second homes. The deduction is made from the taxable gain *before* the 19% CGT is applied. It is hoped that this will stimulate the housing market. To qualify for this relief the property sale must be completed between 1 January 2013 and 31 December 2013. In this scenario, the calculation for the property sale illustrated above would be as follows:

Purchase price	150,000
Transactional costs (*notaire* etc.) at 7.5%	11,250 (150,000 × 7.5%)
Capital improvements @ 15%	22,500 (150,000 × 15%)
Adjusted purchase price	183,750 150,000 + 11,250 + 22,500)
Adjusted gain	36,250 (220,000 – 183,750)
Flat allowance	1,000
Adjusted gain	35,250 (36,250 – 1,000)
8% allowance for years held after first 5 years (4 × 2)	2,820 (35,250 × 8%)
Taxable gain	32,430 (35,250 – 2,820)
Taxable gain after 20% tax relief	25,944 (32,430 – 20%)
Tax @ 19%	4,929

The tax has been reduced from €6,161 to €4,929.

Not so good news

As in the case of Income Tax (Chapter 21) the French social charge of 15.5% is to be added to the capital gain made on the sale of second homes, whether owned by residents or non-residents.

This amounts to 34.5% tax (19% + 15.5%) on any gain, effective retrospectively to August 2012.

This compares unfavourably with the 28% tax take in the UK. If the UK Revenue treats the social charge as, in effect, a tax there would be no tax to pay in the UK (because of the Double Tax Treaty) but the overall cost would be 6.5% higher than it would have been before the change. If, on the other hand, the UK Revenue disregards the social charge paid then an additional 9% would be payable to the UK tax man (28% − 19%). This would bring the overall cost to 43.5% (34.5% + 9%).

As in the case of Income Tax, it remains to be seen whether this proposal will be tested in the courts, as non-French residents can't benefit from the social services paid for by the social charge.

A last minute amendment to the budget proposals introduced another unwelcome swipe at the owners of second homes – *a supplementary tax* (impôt supplémentaire) *on larger capital gains from the sale of second homes.* This is now in force and applies both to residents and non-residents. It should be noted that the tax only affects gains *above €50,000.* Where it applies it is in addition to the CGT of 19% and the social charge of 15.5%. The following is a table of the tax thresholds that will apply:

Table 22.1 Supplementary capital gains tax rates

Gain	Additional tax
50,000–100,000	2%
100,000–150,000	3%
150,000–200,000	4%
200,000–250,000	5%
250,000+	6%

When assessing the likely impact of French CGT on a property investment it is important to remember that **French CGT reduces over time**. UK CGT does not. Indeed, under the new French proposals, if implemented, this reduction will start after just *two years* of ownership (see above). After 5 years, for example, there will be a 15% abatement and after 15 years, 65%. In all likelihood the tax finally paid on the sale of properties held for a reasonable period of time will be broadly the same in both countries.

FORMALITIES FOR NON-RESIDENTS

If the sale price is more than €150,000 an accredited financial agent (*représentant accrédité*) must be appointed to oversee the tax declaration and ensure the correct tax is paid. He effectively guarantees the declaration. The government appointed representative for this purpose is SARF (*société accréditée de representation fiscale*). See Appendix C. Unfortunately the services of SARF do not come cheap – 1% of the sale price. It is possible, however, to use anyone with the right qualifications and accreditation to do this work. The *notaire* acting for the vendor will normally be able to recommend someone.

FORMS AND FILING DEADLINES

The process in France is fast, simple and painful. The *notaire* completes tax declaration form 2090 on behalf of the vendor (even if there is no taxable gain) and withholds any tax due at the point of sale. The vendor never sees it! The *notaire*'s fee for this service (around €70) is paid by the vendor.

The capital gain must also be declared in the UK and here the formalities are rather less hurried. A standard self-assessment form (obtained from the tax payer's regional tax office) is completed, along with the supplementary Capital Gains Pages (form SA108) and the supplementary Foreign Pages (SA106). In the Capital Gains Pages the gain is declared (in sterling) and the tax calculated according to UK revenue rules. In the Foreign Pages the tax paid in France is declared and a claim made for foreign tax credit relief. If the UK tax liability is greater than the French the difference will be due to the UK revenue. If it is less, however, no refund is due.

The deadline for filing is 31 October (for paper-based returns) and 31 January (for online returns) in the year following the tax year in which the gain was made. The forms should be returned to the taxpayer's own tax office.

23

Holiday Letting and UK Tax

In the UK furnished holiday letting (FHL) has always been treated differently by the Revenue from other kinds of residential letting. Unlike long-term letting, it could, potentially, be regarded by the Revenue as a business or *trade*, with significant tax benefits not otherwise available. Holiday letting in the EEA (European Economic Area), however, did not qualify for the same favourable treatment. As this was clearly discriminatory the Revenue was forced to change its position and from 2009–10 furnished holiday letting in the EEA could qualify for the same special treatment.

For the qualifying holiday letting business the tax benefits are significant, both for Income Tax and CGT. They include the ability to claim *Capital Allowances*, use rental income as *'relevant earnings'* for personal pension contributions, claim *Entrepreneurs' Relief* and *Capital Gains Roll-over Relief* on the sale of the property.

TO QUALIFY AS A FURNISHED HOLIDAY LET (FHL)

The following criteria must be met:

■ The property must be located in the UK or the EEA. The EEA consists of the EU (27 states) plus Norway, Liechtenstein and Iceland.

■ The letting must be *commercial*. The objective must be to run it as a business and make a profit. To this end, separate accounts and records should be kept (separate, that is, from those for other rental properties).

■ The property must be available to let for *210 days* per tax year.

■ It must be actually let for at least *105 days* per tax year.

If the property is let to the same person for more than 31 days this period will not qualify as part of the 105 days required. If lettings in excess of 31 days come to more than 155 days in total in the year then the whole year's lettings will fail to qualify.

Where the business consists of more than one property the Revenue will allow *averaging* to be used in order to meet the required number of days let. If, for example, the days let for three properties are 110, 100 and 105, the second property (100) would not qualify on its own. When the three are taken together, however, the average is 105 and all the properties qualify for that tax year.

Because lettings can fluctuate from year to year it is possible that a property will qualify as an FHL in one year but not in the next. To avoid the complications that would occur under these circumstances the Revenue allows what they call a *period of grace election* to be made.

Under this arrangement if a property meets the letting criteria for one year but not for the second and third, the owner may *elect* to have years two and three treated as qualifying. If the property meets the criteria in year four then the property continues to qualify as a FHL. If it fails to meet the criteria in year four, however, it ceases to be an FHL for tax purposes. Anyone availing themselves of this concession must show that there was a genuine intention to let the property and that it was available to be let for the required number of days in the year (210).

It should be noted that all properties owned in the UK are taxed as one FHL business while those in other EEA states are taxed as a separate business. This would mean, for example, that losses incurred in France could not be set against gains in the UK. Any loss on a property in France is set against gains in France. If there is an overall loss it is carried forward to the next tax year.

As the definition of an FHL is crucial for tax purposes the Revenue will expect records to be kept, showing the number of days available and the number of days let for each property.

INCOME TAX BENEFITS

Unlike other forms of residential letting a qualifying FHL allows the taxpayer to claim capital allowances against tax and to contribute to a personal pension, using the rental income as net relevant earnings.

Capital allowances

With ordinary letting the purchase cost of white goods (fridge, freezer, cooker, washing machine, dishwasher) and furniture cannot be set against tax. All that is available is the wear and tear allowance of 10% (see Chapter 21). The cost of these goods can, however, be claimed if the property is a qualifying FHL (the wear and tear allowance is not available for an FHL).

Pension contributions

In the complicated world of personal pensions contributions can only be made on the basis of *net relevant earnings*. There must be an income from employment or self-employment on which to base the contributions to the pension. Unfortunately, rental income from ordinary lettings does not qualify as *net relevant earnings*. The rental income from an FHL, however, *does* qualify and contributions can be based on the level of this income.

CGT BENEFITS

Any gain on the sale of an investment property is taxable, as we have seen in Chapter 22. If the property is a qualifying FHL, however, the *level* of tax paid can be very different, thanks to *Entrepreneurs' Relief*. In addition, if one FHL is sold and another bought *Capital Gains Roll-over Relief* can be claimed.

Entrepreneurs' Relief

The sale of a business asset is not subject to the usual levels of capital gains tax illustrated in Chapter 22 (18% or 28%). If an FHL meets the required criteria it can be possible to claim Entrepreneurs' Relief and pay just **10%** on the gain. In the example of the property sale illustrated in Chapter 22 the calculations would be as follows:

Purchase price	150,000
Transactional costs	11,250
Capital improvements	22,500
Adjusted purchase price	183,750 (150,000 + 11,250 + 22,500)
Adjusted gain	36,250 (220,000 − 183,750)
CGT allowance	10,600
Taxable gain	25,650 (36,250 − 10,600)
Tax @ 10%	**2,565**

The tax payable would be €2,565 instead of €7,182.

Capital Gains Roll-over Relief

This is a very valuable concession from the Revenue at the point when a business asset is sold and another bought. If some or all of the gain from the sale is used to purchase the asset the tax normally paid on that gain can be deferred until the newly purchased asset is sold.

For the owner of a qualifying FHL this can make a significant difference. Take the following example:

A property, qualifying as an FHL, is sold for €150,000, making a capital gain of €30,000. All the gain is used towards the purchase of another FHL for €200,000. If roll-over relief is claimed, no tax is paid on the €30,000 gain until the second property is sold (at which point the purchase price of the second property is deemed to be €170,000 for capital gains tax purposes).

If only some of the gain is used for the second purchase, relief for the amount of the gain used can be claimed.

Local Taxes

There are two local taxes levied on property owners, whether resident or non-resident – a property tax (*taxe foncière*) and an occupancy tax (*taxe d'habitation*).

TAXE FONCIERE

Broadly similar to Council Tax in the UK, this tax is based on the size and condition of the property and its location. Some local authorities add a separate rubbish collection charge (*taxe d'enlèvement des ordures ménagères*) to the bill. The *taxe foncière* (including any rubbish collection charge) is paid by the owner, not the tenant.

The tax is levied yearly in advance and payable in October. Whoever owns the property on 1 January that year is liable to pay the bill. If the property is sold before the next bill is due then the vendor will have paid too much tax. As a refund is not possible the purchaser will normally compensate the vendor for the amount overpaid. This is not usually a matter handled by the *notaire*. The parties come to their own arrangement. However, it is not something the vendor will forget to raise!

There are two exemptions to this tax which are available to the non-resident as well as the resident property owner:

- No tax is levied for the first two years after a property is built (the two years commencing on 1 January after the year of completion). This also applies where the property has been knocked down and rebuilt. The exemption only applies, however, if notification is made within 90 days of completion to the local public finance centre (*centre des finances publiques*).

- There is no tax to pay in the case of registered tourist properties (*meublés de tourisme*) in certain rural areas designated for regeneration (*zones de revitalization rurale*).

Taxe d'habitation

Strange as it seems there is a tax to pay for occupying a property. Even stranger, the tax may be payable even when it is unoccupied! Unlike the *taxe foncière* the level of this tax is based on the notional rental value of the property (arrived at by a complicated formula) and is not always paid by the owner.

If the property is owner occupied, used as a second home or let on a short-term basis the tax is paid by the owner. If the property is let on a long-term basis, however, the tenant is responsible for the tax. The property must be furnished and habitable (with running water, electricity etc.). If it is then the tax will be incurred even if it is not actually occupied. Like the *taxe foncière* it is levied in October for the whole year and payable by the owner or tenant in occupation on 1 January that year. If the property is sold before the next bill is due the vendor remains responsible for that year's tax.

As the tax is based on the rental value any significant improvements to the property could affect the tax level. Accordingly the owner is obliged to let his tax office know if major works have been carried out.

For the landlord there may be an exemption to the *taxe d'habitation* in the case of registered tourist properties (*meublés de tourisme*) in certain rural areas designated for regeneration (*zones de revitalization rurale*). There are other exemptions for the elderly, the disabled, widows and widowers but they apply only where the property is the principal residence of the taxpayer.

If there is a television in the property a TV licence (*redevance audiovisuelle*) must be bought. In France this is not bought separately. The cost (around €120) is cunningly added to the *taxe d'habitation* and must be paid with it. Only one payment is required even if the taxpayer has more than one property, each with a television. Once a year he receives a form asking him to confirm that he has or has not a television set. The non-resident owner indicates the address of the property which is subject to the licence fee addition.

METHODS OF PAYMENT

For both taxes payments can be made by cheque, annual bank transfer, monthly direct debit or online transfer. A 10% penalty is imposed for late payment.

25

Wealth Tax

Some property owners in France (residents and non-residents alike) may be unfortunate enough to encounter another unwelcome tax – the Wealth Tax (*impôt de solidarité sur la fortune*). For French residents this is a tax on their worldwide assets. The good news for the non-resident, however, is that it only relates to property owned in France.

The French Revenue imposes this tax on the 'household' or *foyer* but its definition of 'household' for this purpose includes those who are single, married, in a civil partnership, divorced, widowed or legally responsible for the assets of minors. Not much wriggle-room there!

The tax is paid annually and is based on the *net* market value of the taxpayer's assets on 1 January in the year of assessment. The important word here is 'net' as debts and liabilities can be used to reduce the tax burden. A property, for example, valued at €300,000 with a mortgage of €150,000 would have a net value of €150,000 for the purpose of wealth tax. Other allowable deductions are bank loans, bank overdrafts, initial payments on work to be carried out, local taxes, the social levy, television licence fees and even the taxpayer's own calculation of income tax due to be paid later that year. Documentary evidence (*pièces justificatives*) must be submitted. The net figure will only be subject to wealth tax if it exceeds the threshold exempt figure for that year – €1,310,000 as set out in the budget for 2013. There is no tax to pay for values below this.

MARKET VALUE

For the property owner the crucial issue is the market value of the property. Surprisingly, the Revenue allows the taxpayer to arrive at this himself. It does, however, provide certain criteria which the taxpayer is expected to take into account:

- The physical condition and location of the building, the number of floors and rooms, architectural features, age, state of maintenance and surface area should be taken into account. If the property is an apartment a valuation by square metre (*evaluation au mètre carré utile*) is permissible. The property's proximity to transport, amenities, commercial centres, airport etc. will also be a factor.

- The market value is also influenced by whether the property is owner-occupied or let (let property having a smaller potential market) and whether it is part of a *copropriété* (see Chapter 7).

- The current state of the property market as a whole will naturally impact on values.

EXEMPTIONS

The Double Tax Treaty is of no assistance to the UK resident as no wealth tax is levied in the UK. On the other hand, it is only the property in France that is subject to the tax.

If a non-resident becomes resident in France there is exemption from the tax, on assets outside France, for a period of five years after he takes up residence (until 31 December of the fifth year). After that he will be subject to tax on his worldwide assets, not just his French assets.

The rental property of the 'professional' landlord registered with the *registre du commerce et des sociétés* (see Chapter 21), is exempt and is not included in the calculation for his wealth tax liability.

TAX RATES

Following the election of the socialist government in 2012 it was inevitable that the wealthiest would be expected to pay more tax. The budget proposals for 2013 swept aside the relatively generous Wealth Tax regime of the previous government and introduced the following table of bands and rates *applicable when the threshold of 1,310,000 is exceeded* (no tax to pay when the net value is under this figure).

Table 25.1   Wealth Tax rates

Up to	800,000			0
	800,001	–	1,310,000	0.50%
	1,310,001	–	2,570,000	0.70%
	2,570,001	–	5,000,000	1.00%
	5,000,001	–	10,000,000	1.25%
Above	10,000,000			1.50%

Example

In the case, therefore, of property with a *net* value (see above) of €2,500,000, the calculation would be:

800,000	0
800,001–1,310,000	2,550 (509,999 × 0.5%)
1,310,001–2,500,000	8,330 (1,189,999 × 0.7%)
Total Wealth Tax due	10,880

FORMS AND FILING DEADLINES

Where Wealth Tax is due the responsibility for making the declaration rests with the individual. Form 2725 (*déclaration d'ISF*) can be downloaded from the Revenue website (www.impots. gouv.fr) or obtained from the *Centre des Impôts des Non-Résidents* (see Appendix C). This should be returned with the tax due.

Filing deadlines are 15 June in the year of assessment for residents and 15 July for EU non-residents. For others the deadline is 1 September. Documentary evidence (*pièces justificatives*) to prove outstanding debts and liabilities (see above) will normally be submitted at the same time. They can, however, be submitted at a later date. Where the filing date for the declaration itself is 15 June the documentary evidence can be submitted by 15 September. For 15 July declarations the date for submission is 15 October. For others the date is 30 November.

26

Inheritance Tax

Inheritance Tax (*droits de succession*) can arise following an inheritance on death. If the deceased was resident for tax purposes in France the tax is levied on his worldwide assets. If he was non-resident it is *only those assets held in France* (typically property) that are taken into account.

The tax is payable by the beneficiary or beneficiaries, depending on the amount that each has received from the deceased's estate. If a beneficiary has received a gift from the deceased within 15 years prior to his death this must also be included for inheritance tax purposes.

There are, however, important exemptions and allowances.

EXEMPTIONS

There is no inheritance tax liability on inheritances between spouses or partners in a civil partnership (*pacte civile de solidarieté* or PACS).

Between brother and sister there is also an exemption provided the beneficiary was single, widowed or divorced at the time of death, was more than 50 at the time and had shared the same address as his sibling for at least five years before the death.

ALLOWANCES

The French do not have one tax-free allowance but several (adjusted annually for inflation), depending on the relationship of the beneficiary to the deceased. For 2012–2013 the principal allowances (*abattements*) are:

Between parents and children	€100,000
Between siblings	€15,932
Between nephews/nieces	€7,967

For the beneficiary who qualifies for none of the above there is an allowance of €1,594.

TAX RATES

Where tax is payable the French Revenue does not levy a flat rate of tax for all. As in the case of the Wealth Tax, a system of tax bands applies. In this case, however, the relationship of beneficiary to deceased is also taken into account. For 2012–2013 the tax rates are as follows:

Table 26.1   Inheritance Tax rates between parents and children

Up to	€8,072	5%
Between	€8,072 and €12,109	10%
Between	€12,109 and €15,932	15%
Between	€15,932 and €552,324	20%
Between	€552,324 and €902,838	30%
Between	€902,838 and €1,805,677	40%
Above	€1,805,677	45%

Table 26.2 Inheritance Tax rates between siblings

Up to	€24,430	35%
Above	€24,430	45%

Other relatives will face a tax bill of 55% (after their tax-free allowance) while non-relatives will pay 60%.

Example

In the case of a child who inherits €250,000 from a parent the first €100,000 (child's allowance) is tax-free. The balance of €150,000 is taxed as follows:

	Tax	
8,072	404	(8,072 × 5%)
4,037 (12,109 – 8,072)	404	(4,037 × 10%)
3,823 (15,932 – 12,109)	573	(3,823 × 15%)
134,068 (150,000 – 15,932)	26,814	(134,068 × 20%)
Total tax due	28,195	

FILING DEADLINES AND PAYMENT

If the deceased was resident in France the beneficiaries must make a declaration through a *notaire* within six months of the death. In the case of a non-resident the time allowed is 12 months.

Payment can be made in cash or by cheque. Where prior agreement has been obtained certain works of art, buildings in certain conservation areas or shares in quoted companies can be accepted in payment. In some circumstances payment can be delayed (e.g. when the beneficiary does not have the legal right to dispose of a property) or paid in instalments for a period of up to five years, where an acceptable guarantee can be provided.

The Double Tax Treaty with the UK ensures that inheritance tax is not levied twice on a UK resident.

Sample Holiday Let Contract and Booking Terms

Please note. These are not definitive versions of a contract and booking terms. Adjustments will need to be made to suit individual circumstances (e.g. in relation to the cancellation policy, deposits, rules regarding pets etc.). Please also note that this is not a legal document and legal advice should be taken in the drafting of the contract and booking terms.

Holiday Letting Contract
Furnished rental of

Property address

_____

_____

Between

The Landlord   *Name and Address*

_____

_____

The Tenant(s)

Name and address of lead tenant

_____

_____

Phone number _____

Mobile number _____

Email _____

Names of other members of party

_____

_____

Total in party   _____

Arrival date   _____
Departure date   _____

Rent   _____
Additional costs   _____
Deposit   _____
Date balance due   _____
Payment method   _____

I have read, understood and accept the attached Booking Terms
and Conditions. I am over 18 and confirm that the property will
be rented for the dates specified in this contract only and that the
property will not constitute my principal residence. I am signing
this contract on behalf of myself and all members of the party.

Lead Tenant   *Signature*   *Date*

                   _____   _____

Landlord   *Signature*   *Date*

                   _____   _____

BOOKING TERMS AND CONDITIONS

Confirmation of booking

The booking is confirmed when the signed contract and deposit are received and acceptance acknowledged in writing by the owner. The contract can be emailed, faxed or posted. For payment options, see below.

Deposit and payment

For bookings made more than eight weeks before the start of the holiday, a non-refundable deposit of . . . . is required at the time of booking. The balance will be due 8 weeks before the commencement of the holiday. The owners reserve the right to re-let the property in the event of non-payment by the due date. For bookings made less than 8 weeks before commencement full payment is required.

Method of payment

Payment can be in GB pounds or (by prior agreement as to the currency and the amount) in another currency. Payment can be made by:

- personal cheque (by prior agreement)

- bank draft, bank transfer, online transfer within the UK

- bank transfer from outside the UK

- PayPal

- credit card or debit card

Security deposit

A refundable deposit will be required to cover breakages, losses and any *exceptional* cleaning. The property will be cleaned after you leave but if it is left in a particularly dirty condition, requiring additional cleaning, a suitable amount will be deducted from the deposit to cover the extra cost involved. The deposit (less any deductions applicable) will be returned within 14 days of the return of the keys.

Number of occupants

This must not exceed the number stated in the contract.

Pets

Pets are not allowed.

Damage

You agree not to damage the property, its furniture, fittings and fixtures in any way.

Nuisance

You agree not to cause a nuisance that would disturb other occupants of the building or neighbouring buildings.

Cancellation and refunds

Within 4 weeks of the first night booked, no refund except for security deposit. Between 4 and 8 weeks of the first night booked 50% of rental value plus security deposit.

Arrival and departure times

Check-in and check-out times must be observed:

Check-in: after 14:30

Check-out: before 11:00

Key collection

Instructions for key collection are provided separately. These must be strictly followed.

Travel insurance

Comprehensive cover for all party members is strongly advised. This insurance should cover costs incurred due to cancellation, interruption of holiday, medical treatment and public liability. The owners cannot accept liability for these.

Problems during your stay

While it is hoped your stay will be trouble-free if you do have problems it is essential to notify us or our agent immediately so that matters can be put right without delay.

Legal jurisdiction

This contract is subject to the law of England and Wales. The parties to the contract agree that any dispute arising from the contract will be dealt with exclusively by the English and Welsh courts.

Glossary of French words and phrases

BANKING

carte à autorisation systématique	debit card requiring each transaction to be authorised
carte bleue	debit card
carte de séjour	residency permit
carte d'identité	identity card
chèque	cheque
chéquier	cheque book
clé RIB	bank account code
code banque	sort code
code guichet	branch code
code secret	secret code
compte à vue	current account
compte de dépôt	current account
compte non-résident	non-resident account
conseiller clientèle	relationship manager
convention de compte	account agreement

découvert	overdraft
distributeur	ATM
interdiction bancaire	ban on using cheques
numéro client	client number
numéro de compte	account number
ouvrir un compte	open an account
prélèvement automatique	direct debit
récapitulatif annuel des frais bancaires	annual statement of bank charges
relevé de compte	bank statement
relevé d'identité bancaire	statement of full bank details
titre interbancaire de payment (TIP)	permission to debit an account
virement	bank transfer
virgule	comma (instead of decimal point)

CO-OWNERSHIP

carnet d'entretien	maintenance report
feuille de présence	attendance sheet
frais faibles	low management charges
millièmes	thousandths
procès-verbal	minutes of meeting
quote-part	share of apartment building
règlement de copropriété	rules of the co-ownership
syndic	management company for the copropriété
tantième	percentage

Inheritance planning

attribution de la communauté au survivant	leaving property to the survivor under a *communauté universelle* marriage regime
communauté universelle	matrimonial regime under which assets are held jointly
Convention de la Haye	Hague Convention
droits de succession	inheritance tax
en indivision	split ownership (tenancy in common)
en tontine	tontine or joint ownership
quotité disponible	portion of estate which can be left to anyone
réserve légale	portion of estate which must be left to immediate family
séparation des biens	matrimonial regime under which assets are held separately
Société Civile Immobilière (SCI)	company for holding property
tontine	tontine

Insurance

abandon de recours	the insurer undertakes not to pursue the tenant in the event of a claim
assurance décès	life insurance
assurance décès-invalidité	life and disability cover
assurance dommages-ouvrages	insurance policy for developer's ten-year guarantee

assurance en responsabilité civile professionnelle	indemnity insurance
assurance groupe	group insurance policy
assurance loyers impayés	insurance against unpaid rent
clauses personnalisées	endorsements
contrat d'assurances externe	life insurance policy not arranged through the mortgage lender
cotisation à échéance	premium due
courtier en assurances	insurance broker
exclusion médicale	exclusion for medical reasons in a life insurance policy
formulaire d'assurance	insurance application form
franchise	excess
garantie incapacité temporaire de travail	temporary illness cover
garantie invalidité permanente totale	total and permanent disability cover
garantie responsibilité civile	public liability insurance
incendie, explosions, dégâts des eaux	fire, explosion and floods
l'assurance de chose suit la chose	'the insurance follows the thing' – meaning subsequent purchasers are also covered
mobilier	contents
montant assuré	sum assured
multirisque habitation	standard property insurance
police d'assurance	insurance policy
primes d'assurance	insurance premium
questionnaire de santé	health questionnaire

recours des voisins et des tiers	third party liability
résiliation	cancellation of policy
souscrire une assurance	take out a policy
surprime	premium loading
valeur à neuf	new for old

LETTING

à échoir	in advance
à effet de serre	greenhouse effect (part of Energy Performance certificate required by law)
à terme échu	in arrears
amendes	fines for breach of contract
bail	tenancy agreement
ballon	water heater
blanchisserie	laundry
caution	guarantee
caution solidaire	a guarantee binding on all parties/a third-party guarantee
chaudière	central heating boiler
clause résolutoire	clause stating conditions for voiding a contract
clause solidaire	clause making tenants jointly liable
concubin/e	common law husband/wife
congé	notice
congé pour vente	notice to sell
contrat de bail	tenancy agreement

dépôt de garantie	deposit
dégradation	damage
délai de préavis	notice period
dératisation	pest control (rats)
désinsectisation	pest control (insects)
droit de préemption	right of pre-emption
épis	ears of corn (*Gîtes de France* classification)
état des lieux	inventory
état des lieux contradictoire	inventory signed by both parties
étiquette	label for energy efficiency
femme de ménage	housekeeper
garantie des risques locatifs	insurance against risks associated with letting
garantie locative	insurance against unpaid rent
gestion immobilière	property letting and management
gestionnaire immobilier	letting and management agent
huissier de justice	court bailiff
Indice du Coût de la Construction	Cost of Construction Index
lettre recommandée avec accusé de réception	registered letter to be signed for
location meublée	furnished letting
location saisonnière	holiday letting
location vide	unfurnished letting
logement décent	acceptable accommodation
loué	let
loueur en meublé professionnel	professional landlord of furnished property

loyers de référence	comparable rents
meublés de tourisme	furnished tourist accommodation
pièces justificatives	documentary evidence (for tenant references)
planning	schedule
redevance audiovisuelle	television licence
résidences de tourisme	government approved holiday complexes
résiliation	termination of contract
revenu minimum d'insertion	Income support
révision du loyer	rent review
salaire minimum interprofessionnel de croissance (SMIC)	minimum wage
siège social	company head office
sous-location	subletting
tacite reconduction	automatic renewal
vétusté	dilapidation

Letting Agents

mandant	principal in an agency agreement
mandat avec exclusivité	sole agency
mandat d'administration de biens	letting and management agreement
mandat de gestion locative	letting and management agreement
mandataire	person with power of attorney or agent in agency agreement
sans exclusivité	not a sole agency

MORTGAGES

contrat d'épargne	savings plan
courtier en prêts	mortgage broker
formulaire de demande de prêt	mortgage application form
frais de courtier	mortgage broker's fee
frais de dossier	arrangement fee
hypothèque conventionnelle	conventional mortgage
mainlevée	mortgage release
offre préalable d'un crédit immobilier	preliminary mortgage offer
pénalités de remboursement anticipé	early redemption penalties
prêt	loan
prêt immobilier	mortgage
prêt in fine	interest only mortgage
prêt classique/prêt amortissable	repayment mortgage
prêt à taux fixe	rate mortgage
prêt à taux revisable	variable rate mortgage
privilège de prêteur de deniers	first charge mortgage
sans crédit	no mortgage required
taux effectif global du prêt (TEG)	global effective rate

PROPERTY DESCRIPTION/LETTING ADVERTS

à louer	to let
agréable	pleasant
aperçu mer	sea view
arrondissement (arr)	district
ascenseur (asc)	lift/elevator

au calme	peaceful
balcon	balcony
ballon	water heater
canapé	sofa-bed
cave	cellar
chambre (ch)	bedroom
chasse d'eau	toilet cistern
chaudière	central heating boiler
chauffage collectif	communal heating
chauffage électrique	electric heating
chauffage gaz	gas heating
chauffage individual	independent heating
climatisation	air conditioning
coin cuisine	small kitchen area in lounge
complètement rénové,	completely renovated
concièrge	concierge
cuisine aménagée	fitted kitchen
cuisine americaine	open-plan kitchen
cuisine équipée	equipped kitchen
cuisine indépendante	separate kitchen
cuisine séparée	separate kitchen
cuisinière	cooker/stove
dernier étage	top floor
digicode	digital lock
double vitrage	double glazing
en parfait état	in perfect condition
ensoleillé	bright and sunny

entrée	hall
étage (et)	floor/storey
étudiants boursiers	grant-aided students
évier	kitchen sink
exposition (expo) sud	south facing
foyers d'étudiants	student hostel accommodation
gardien	caretaker
idéal étudiant	suit student
immeuble recent	new building
interphone	interphone
libre immédiatement	available immediately
loyer	rent
loyer charges comprises (cc)	rent with charges included
lumineux	bright
meublé	furnished
meublé ou vide	furnished or unfurnished
mezzanine	mezzanine floor
parking	parking
parlophone	interphone
particulier	private individual
passer une annonce	place an advertisement
petites annonces	small ads
pièces	rooms
piscine	swimming pool
placards	cupboards
plaques	hot plates
plaques électriques	electric hotplates

proches toutes commodities	close to all amenities
quartier	district
refait à neuf	newly refurbished
réfrigérateur (frigo)	fridge
rez-de-chausée (rdc)	ground floor
salle d'eau	shower room
salle de bains	bathroom
salle de douche	shower room
sans ascensceur	no lift
securisé	secure/safe
séjour (séj)	lounge
standing	luxury
studio	studio
sur cour	overlooking courtyard
tarifs	prices (for placing an advert)
terrasse	terrace/large balcony
traversant	windows on street and courtyard
très bien meublé	very well furnished
très bon état	very good condition
ventilateur	extractor fan
vue dégagée	unobstructed view
vue mer	sea view
WC séparé	separate toilet

PROPERTY PURCHASE

à la commission	on commission
à usage mixte	for residential and business

absence de restriction à son droit de disposer	no restriction on right to sell
acquéreur	purchaser
acte de vente	final contract of sale
acte sous seing privé	private agreement
administrateur de biens	letting and management agent
agences immobilières	estate agencies
agent immobilier	estate agent
amiante	asbestos
attestation	certificate to confirm completion of purchase
barème	scale of fees
bureau des hypothèques	land registry office
carnet d'entretien	maintenance record
carte professionnelle	estate agent's licence
charte de déontologie des chasseurs immobiliers	professional code of conduct for property finders
chasseur immobilier	property finder
clause par équivalent	clause in the final contract allowing a developer to use equivalent or similar materials
clause suspensive	conditional clause in contract of sale
code d'éthique et de déontologie	professional code of conduct
commission comprise	commission included
compromis de vente	preliminary contract
compte client	client account opened by *notaire*

conditions suspensives	conditions to be met before a contract is binding
constat	full report
contrat de réservation	preliminary contract for off-plan purchase
copie authentique	authenticated copy of final contract
copropriété	co-ownership
copropriétaire	co-owner/apartment owner
débours	*notaire*'s disbursements
défaut de conformité	failure on the developer's part to provide exactly what is specified in the contract
délai de rétractation	cooling-off period in a contract
dépôt de garantie	initial deposit in an off-plan purchase/tenancy deposit
diagnostic immobilier de performance énergétique (DPE)	energy performance rating
droit commun	statutory rights
émoluments proportionnels	variable fees
entretien	maintenance
état de frais	*notaire*'s completion statement
evaluation au mètre carré utile	valuation based on surface area
frais de notaire	legal costs
garantie d'achèvement	guarantee of completion
garantie de parfait-achèvement	developer's one-year guarantee
garantie de remboursement	refund guarantee
garantie des éléments d'équipements	developer's two-year guarantee
garantie extrinsèque	guarantee by a third party

garantie intrinsèque	personal guarantee
géomètre	surveyor
honoraires	fees
honoraires du notaire	*notaire*'s fees
impropre à sa destination	unfit for purpose
isolation phonique	sound proofing
mandat de recherche	purchaser's agreement with property finder
mandat de vente	vendor's agreement with estate agent
net vendeur	sale price less the agent's commission
notaire	notary
notice descriptif	detailed account of planned construction
offre d'achat	offer to buy
prix net	price excluding agent's fee
procuration	power of attorney
promesse d'achat	offer to buy
promesse de vente	preliminary contract
promoteur immobilier	property developer
rendement brut	gross yield
rendement net	net yield
saturnisme	lead poisoning
superficie	floor area
termites	termites
tribunal d'instance	civil court
vendeur	vendor

vente en l'état futur d'achèvement (VEFA)	selling off-plan
vice de construction	bad workmanship
zones de revitalization rurale	rural areas earmarked for regeneration

TAX

abattement	tax-free allowance
brut	gross
centre des finances publiques	public finance centre
décote	tax relief
droits de succession	inheritance tax
fiscalement domiciliées en France	resident in France for tax purposes
foyer	household
impôt de solidarité sur la fortune	wealth tax
impôt sur les plus-values	capital gains tax
micro-foncier	the simplified tax regime for unfurnished lettings
pacte civile de solidarité (PACS)	civil partnership
pension de vieillesse	old age pension
pièces justificatives	documentary evidence
régime réel	tax regime for rental income that takes actual expenses into account
TVA (taxe sur la valeur ajoutée)	VAT (Value Added Tax)
taxe d'enlèvement des ordures ménagères	rubbish collection tax

taxe d'habitation	occupancy tax
taxe de publicité foncière	stamp duty
taxe foncière	local property tax
toutes taxes comprises (TTC)	inclusive of tax

Useful Addresses

ADVERTISING FOR LANDLORDS

www.topannonces.fr
(website only, free for private advertisers)

www.paruvendu.fr
(website only or website + newspaper)

www.jannonce.fr
(website only or website + newspaper, one week free for private advertisers)

www.immo-sur-cartes.com
(website only, free for adverts without photos)

www.explorimmo.com
(website only)

www.cliczoom.com
(website only)

www.entreparticuliers.com
private advertisers only, no agents

www.pap.fr
(website or website + *Particulier à Particulier* newspaper)
www.crous-paris.fr
(student market)

CLEANERS AND AGENTS/WHERE TO FIND

http://geo.craigslist.org/iso/fr

http://www.angloinfo.com

http://jobs.justlanded.com

http://www.franglo.com

http://menage.vivastreet.fr/annonces-menage

ENERGY PERFORMANCE ASSESSORS

Agence de l'Environnement et de la Maîtrise de l'Energie
http://www.ademe.fr

ENGLISH-SPEAKING NOTARIES

www.notaires.fr

Click on 'rechercher un notaire'. In the field 'ville ou code postal' type
the name of the town or city. In the field 'langue pratiquée' choose
'Anglais' from the drop-down menu.

ESTATE AGENTS' PROFESSIONAL BODIES

Fédération Nationale de l'Immobilier (FNAIM)
http://www.fnaim.fr/

Syndicat National des Professionnels Immobiliers (SNPI)
http://www.snpi.com/

FNAIM
(Fédération Nationale de l'Immobilier)
29, rue du Faubourg Saint-Honoré
75008 PARIS
Tel: 01 44 20 77 00
www.fnaim.fr

FPC (Fédération Des Promoteurs Constructeurs De France)
106 Rue De L Universite, Paris, Paris 75007
Tel: 0147054436
Fax: 0147539273
http://www.fnpc.fr

FOREIGN EXCHANGE DEALERS

TTT Moneycorp Ltd
100 Brompton Road, Knightsbridge, London, SW3 ER
Tel: 0207 823 7500
http://www.moneycorp.com

Foreign Currency Exchange
3 Progression Centre, Mark Road, Hemel Hempstead,
Herts, UK, HP2 7DW
Tel: (freephone for UK callers) 0800 783 4313
Other callers + 44 (0)1442 233 040
Fax: + 44(0) 1442 241 850
http://www.fcexchange.co.uk

Currencies Direct Limited
Hanover House, 73/74 High Holborn, London, WC1V 6LS
Tel: 0207 813 0332
Fax: 0207 419 7753
http://www.currenciesdirect.com/

FRENCH BANKS

BNP Paribas
http://www.bnpparibas.com/en/home/default.asp

Credit Mutuel
https://www.creditmutuel.fr/cmo/fr/info/accueil/anglais/index.html

Barclays
http://www.barclays.fr

HSBC
http://www.hsbc.fr

Banque Populaire
http://www.banquepopulaire.fr
http://www.cotedazur.banquepopulaire.fr

Crédit Agricole
http://www.credit-agricole.fr
http://www.britline.com

Crédit Lyonnais
https://www.lcl.fr

GITES DE FRANCE

http://www.gites-de-france.com

HELP FOR TENANTS

La Caisse d'Allocations Familiales (CAF)
https://www.caf.fr

Action Logement
http://www.uesl.fr/

Conseil d'administration du Comité Interprofessionnel du Logement
(CIL)
http://www.cipl43.fr

Conseil d'administration de l'UESL (Fédération d'Action Logement)
http://www.uesl.fr

GRL Gestion
http://www.grlgestion.fr

HIGH RISK LIFE COVER

AERAS
http://www.aeras-infos.fr/
Address for appeals:
Commission de médiation de la convention AERAS
61 rue Taitbout
75009 PARIS

HOLIDAY LET AGENCIES OFFERING FULL MANAGEMENT

http://www.interhome.com

https://www.french-country-cottages.co.uk

http://www.parisaddress.com

HOLIDAY LET WEBSITES FOR OWNERS

http://www.holiday-rentals.co.uk/

http://www.holidaylettings.co.uk/

http://www.ownersdirect.co.uk/

HOLIDAY LET SPECIALIST INSURERS (UK)

Schofields Underwriting Agencies
Trinity House
7 Institute Street
Bolton BL1 1PZ
Tel: 01204 365080
http://www.schofields.ltd.uk/

Intasure
Suffolk House
George Street
Croydon CRO 1PE
Tel: 0208 274 6778
http://intasure.com/

INFORMATION FOR LANDLORD AND TENANT

Agence Nationale pour l'information sur le logement (ANIL)
http://www.anil.org/fr/index.html

INTERNET/CABLE TV

Numericable
www.numericable.fr

LEGAL COSTS CALCULATION

http://www.immobilier.notaires.fr/jahia/Jahia/immobilier/guest/calcul/fraisAcquisition

Mortgage brokers (UK)
Conti
First floor, Sheridan House,
112–116 Western Road,
Hove
East Sussex BN3 1DD
Tel: +44 (0) 1273 772811
Fax: +44 (0) 1273 321269
http://www.mortgagesoverseas.com/

Savills Private Finance
25 Finsbury Circus,
London EC2M 7EE
Tel: +44 (0) 20 7330 8500
Fax: +44 (0) 20 7330 8501
http://www.spf.co.uk/

MORTGAGE LENDERS

Barclays
http://www.woolwich.co.uk/mortgages/buying-abroad.html

BNP Paribas International Buyers
http://www.bnpparibas-pf-french-mortgage.com/

Crédit Agricole
http://www.credit-agricole.fr/particuliers/financements/credit-immobilier/

Crédit Foncier
http://www.creditfoncier.co.uk
http://www.creditfoncier.fr

Crédit Immobilier
http://www.credit-immobilier-de-france.fr/

CIC (Crédit Industriel et Commercial)
https://www.cic.fr/en/bank/personal-banking/banking-services/
mortgages/index.html
Tel: + 33 03 83 97 89 37

Crédit Lyonnais (LCL)
LCL, 55 Champs Elysées,75008 Paris
Tel: +33 142 950 438
http://particuliers.lcl.fr/prets/buying-a-home-in-france/#

HSBC
www.hsbc.co.uk/1/2/personal/mortgages/buy-overseas

La Poste (la Banque Postale)
http://www.post.be/site/fr/postoffice/financialServices/mortgage_loan.
html

PayPal

www.paypal.com

PROPERTY FINDERS' PROFESSIONAL BODIES

Fédération Nationale des Chasseurs Immobiliers (FNCI)
http://www.fnci.fr/

La Fédération Française des Chasseurs Immobiliers (FFCI)
http://www.federation-chasseurs-immobiliers.com/

RENTAL INSURANCE FOR LANDLORDS

http://www.cornhill.fr/

http://www.credit-agricole.fr

http://www.assuranceloyersimpayes.com

http://www.sacapp.com

http://particuliers.lcl.fr

RENT INCREASE

Institut national de la statistique et des études economiques (INSEE)
http://www.insee.fr/fr/themes/conjoncture/indice_loyer.asp

Union National de la Propriété Immobiliére (UNPI)
http://www.unpi13.org/index.html

SARF (Société Accréditée de Representation Fiscale)
2 Rue Petits Pères, 75002 Paris
Tel: 01 42 44 22 33

SNRT (Syndicat National des Résidences de Tourisme)
177 Avenue Achille
Perretti 92200
Neuilly sur Seine
Tel: 01 47 38 35 60
Fax: 01 47 38 35 61
Email: snrt@snrt.fr

STATE HELP FOR LANDLORDS

Agence Nationale de l'Habitat (ANAH)
http://www.anah.fr

TAX

French tax returns
Centre des Impôts des Non-Résidents (CINR)
TSA 10010
10 rue du Centre
93465 Noisy-le-Grand Cedex
France
Tel: +33 (0)1 57 33 83 00
Fax: +33 (0)1 57 33 82 66
Email: nonresidents@dgfip.finances.gouv.fr
www.impots.gouv.fr

UK Revenue
www.hmrc.gov.uk

TENANCY AGREEMENTS

www.tissot.fr

WEBSITES FOR MEDIUM-TERM TENANTS

http://www.french-locations.co.uk/

http://www.rentaplaceinfrance.com

http://www.yourgateway2france.com

YELLOW PAGES

http://www.pagesjaunes.fr/

Index